RICHARD CRASHAW: A STUDY IN STYLE AND POETIC DEVELOPMENT

A Lemma Publishing Corporation Reprint Edition

This Lemma Publishing Corporation edition of Ruth C. Wallerstein's *Richard Crashaw: A Study in Style and Poetic Development* is an unabridged republication of the first edition, published in Madison, Wisconsin in 1935 as *University of Wisconsin Studies in Language and Literature,* No. 37.

International Standard Book Number 0-87696-036-0
Library of Congress Catalog Card Number 74-180775

Published by
Lemma Publishing Corporation
509 Fifth Avenue
New York, N.Y. 10017

Printed in U.S.A.

UNIVERSITY OF WISCONSIN STUDIES
IN LANGUAGE AND LITERATURE
NUMBER 37

# RICHARD CRASHAW
# A STUDY IN STYLE AND POETIC DEVELOPMENT

BY

RUTH C. WALLERSTEIN

ASSISTANT PROFESSOR OF ENGLISH
UNIVERSITY OF WISCONSIN

MADISON
1935

To

MY FATHER

1863-1932

## CONTENTS

# PREFACE

The friends and colleagues to whom I am indebted for interest and for valuable stimulation in the course of the preparation of the book are more than those whose names can appear in this list of particular obligations. My friend Miss F. Louise Nardin read my first draft and had many invaluable suggestions to make. The members of the Committee on Publications of the English Department of the University of Wisconsin, Professors J. F. A. Pyre, William Ellery Leonard, and Julia Grace Wales, each read my book with great care, and each made important suggestions. I am most warmly grateful to them both for their interest and for their help. This is but one among numerous occasions recently on which I have turned to Professor Pyre, and on which he has shown unfailing generosity and interest. Professors Arthur Beatty and Helen C. White were also good enough to read the typescript. I am grateful to the keeper of the Printed Books of the British Museum and to the Keeper of Manuscripts of the Museum for permission to use their resources, and to Bodley's Librarian and to the Librarian of the Public Library of New York City, and especially to the Librarian of the Rare Book Room of that library for the same kind permission. Mr. Butterfield, then librarian of Peterhouse College in Cambridge, allowed me to consult books and manuscripts there in 1930. Mr. Walter Smith, our University Librarian, has been helpful in borrowing books for me. Miss Hester Meigs verified several citations for me in the Public Library of New York City. Mr. Mark Schorer has given me generous and most valuable aid in proofreading. Mrs. Paul Clark helped to make the index.

To the Regents of the University of Wisconsin, and through them to the State of Wisconsin, I most gratefully acknowledge my deep obligation for their generous provisions by which the final copy of my book has been typed and the book printed and published.

My earliest, deepest, and most continuous debt in all my study of literature I owe to one whom I cannot now thank. I have tried to express my sense of that among other uncounted obligations in my dedication.

RUTH WALLERSTEIN.

Madison, November 1933.

## Chapter I

# INTRODUCTORY

**Poet and Saint! to thee alone are given**
**The two most sacred names of earth and heaven;**

In no poet are the art and the inner development more deeply bound up in each other than in Richard Crashaw. He passed through a series of poetic influences each of which shaped almost violently his thought and his artistic expression. As a school-boy he was trained in the conventional, formal themes and in the highly artificial rhetoric of the neo-Latin and neo-Greek epigram; and in this form he produced a considerable amount of work remarkable among the large body of such epigrams for its skill and even at times for its power in its own kind, and no less signal in that he alone of the numerous English poets who must have been similarly drilled created anything of importance in the mode, or felt it as an abiding influence. Marino was the next influence and a powerful one. And then he made an intensive study of the craft of emblem and *impresa.* In none of these studies, however, violently as they wrenched his style, was Crashaw concerned merely or primarily with style. In his study of rhetoric, emblem, *impresa,* a dual process of mind was going on. The study was for Crashaw, as we shall see, a kind of intellectual discipline akin, in the artistic realm, to the discipline, in the intellectual realm, of mastering the technique of meditation. And yet in the early stages his style remains fantastic and artificial. It is only as his inner life lays hold upon us that we can understand how the ingenious, theatrical, often trivial and barbarous elements of that style became at last fused and transmuted into poetic utterance. And, on the other hand, so alien from the main stream of our poetic style, so special, so esoteric in his expression is Crashaw in all but his supreme passages, that only after we have come through intensive study to understand his mode of expression will he yield in full his poetic vision. And yet, though his manner seem esoteric, the chemistry by which vision and style grew into poetry is universal and central; to understand Crashaw's poetic development is to move far into the centre of the mystery of poetry.

Whether we view him as poet or "saint," he is an intense and moving figure. If one could have had a portrait of him—and could have shifted time a little to secure one's full desire—one would have wished it to be done by El Greco. He seems, as do all such passionate natures so intently focused, to have flashed across a vast arc of life in some rare light, while quieter natures are moving their set miles down accustomed ways. The son of an Anglican divine of Puritan tendencies, he ultimately entered the Catholic church. As a figure among the exiles of the Civil War in Paris we have only one direct glimpse of him, but a glimpse full of meaning. Among the courtiers and cavaliers working fitfully for the cause of Charles II as they found opportunity, and amusing themselves profusely in their enforced idleness from accustomed responsibilities, he had, of course, no part. But neither do we hear of him among the men of letters and scholars—of whom his friend Cowley was one—who penetrated into the intellectual life of Paris, and were busy with philosophy and with problems of literary criticism and literary creation, preparing, during the Exile, for their part in the transformation of English literature to the spirit of reason. Standing apart, "Par le bon example de sa vie il a beaucoup edifié tous ceux qui ont conversé avec luy." His poetic development is equally dramatic. Of the fairly small body of poetry which he wrote in his half-life—for he had only thirty-six of the three score years and ten—much is imperfectly realized and entangled in the web of its techniques, and some, indeed, remains as the very model of bad taste in poetry; but the few perfectly realized poems and passages, such as the *Hymn in the Nativity*, or the last lines on St. Teresa, stand in intensity of meaning and in magic beauty with the supreme things of English verse. At an early age, in some passages in the *Sospetto d' Herode*, he had so mastered the style and feeling of Spenser that in a few stanzas he seems to stand on the heights with Spenser himself above all the Spenserians, the heir who should carry on the work of Spenser in its full scope. But upon this assured and perfected style he deliberately turned his back, to serve an apprenticeship among the sterile theatricalities of Marino and among the turgid intellectualities of minor neo-Latin religious writers. But while as a craftsman he was thus at work on these superficial models, in the development of his personal life Crashaw was concentrating upon some of the profound masters of that religious way to which he had begun to devote himself; and his poetic art did not remain uninfluenced by his whole imaginative development.

It is with Crashaw's poetic development, and specifically with his style, that we are concerned. But his life and his mental development are central in our understanding of the moulding of his art; his art can, indeed, be fully understood only in the light of that maturing of the imagination which ultimately shaped it, turning a system of techniques in truth into a style. Our second chapter, therefore, will set forth Crashaw's life and intellectual history.

Crashaw's poetic development was, as we have already suggested, a highly self-conscious and educated one, involving a minute study of techniques and a careful drill in them. This study drew from a number of widely different sources. And the schools of poetry in which he was early trained and later trained himself as an apprentice had very formal rhetorical laws and very formal modes of image-making, based on complex and conventionalized intellectual patterns. Their techniques defined and ordered the units of design, the elements of expression, as impersonally, as abstractly and scientifically, as does the Japanese art of floral arrangement. In the case of Crashaw's poetry the counted flower stems and blossoms with which he built his design were, first, particular forms of metaphor and special tropes, and then a scheme of symbolism which is peculiarly esoteric because it often uses as its symbols words and objects with very minutely particularized individual connotations. He spent his early years learning to make and to use these symbols.

A large body of his work belongs to his apprenticeship. And since much of this work consists of imitations and translations, his masters are well known to us: they are the neo-Latin epigrammatists and elegists, and in special among these the religious writers; the rhetorics and rhetorical handbooks which expressed the theory of these writers; Marino and the Marinisti; and the classical Latin and Greek poets and the Alexandrians, whom Crashaw translated in a few fugitive pieces. The general course of his apprenticeship, too, is clear, though its detailed outlines are obscure. Crashaw brought up to Pembroke College from his school days at Charterhouse a reputation as a promising young poet. And we know from our general knowledge of the course of studies in the preparatory school of his time that his poetic training was likely to consist in the writing of Latin and Greek epigrams on set Biblical themes such as we actually find in Crashaw's first published work. Thus, though we do not know whether any of the verse in this first published volume of 1635 was indeed the product of his boyhood, we may be sure that the study of this epigrammatic form, and probably also of the rhetorical handbook that paid so much attention to the form, constituted the first stage of his apprenticeship. In his early under-graduate years, the classical poets are likely to have been an important part of his studies; but his translations from these poets show so little of the spirit of the originals and so much of Marinism and the method of the epigram that we can hardly account the originals as significant forces in the creation of Crashaw's art. Marino and to some extent the Marinisti form the serious study of the second step in Crashaw's development,—a study in which he was engrossed during his later undergraduate years. These forces did not act upon Crashaw merely as general and pervasive influences, he served to them conscientiously the full term of his indenture. Our first task, therefore, in the study of Crawshaw's style must be a detailed analysis of his epigrams and of his Marinistic poems and the relation of these poems to their models. To understand to the full the significance of these forms, we must study both the techniques themselves and Crashaw's use and transformation of them. We must seek, that is, to isolate and define the special techniques present in Crashaw's work; and, when we have thus defined them, we must see how, at every stage, Crashaw's art informed and filled them. Chapter III then will be devoted to a study of Crashaw's epigrams against the background of the neo-Latin epigram in general and the rhetorics. Chapter IV will consider his translations and imitations, particularly those of Marino. Into this fourth chapter also still another problem will enter. For at the same time that he was exercising himself in these special foreign forms, he was also influenced by poetry of a very different mode. The

English poetry of the time was strongly at work upon his imagination, and particularly the poetry of Spenser, who exerted upon Crashaw, as upon so many poets, a force that shaped the very heart and manner of his verse. And this influence shows itself very powerfully in the translation from Marino. It will, accordingly, form part of our study of that translation. The next formative influences upon Crashaw were those of emblem and *impresa*; and in a more general way the symbolism of church ritual and church art. This latter influence (the symbolism was itself often stylized and elaborated by the same intellectual impulse that created the neo-Latin epigram) is so diffused that it cannot be specifically defined at any one point, but must be taken account of throughout. To emblem and *impresa* also Crashaw served a less formal apprenticeship than to epigram, rhetoric, and Marinism although their influence upon him was more specific than that of church art. Rather, they helped to clarify and concentrate his movement in the direction in which he was already going. And we must trace their general imaginative influence upon his method and spirit rather than look for their formative power in a specific body of verse; for Crashaw used only two or three emblem designs and wrote only one or two emblems to illustrate other poems. In the circumstances, it is impossible to fix even an approximate date for the central period of their influence upon him, although there is some evidence to show that he paid special attention to them during that portion of his exile which he passed in Holland. We may say then that our fundamental definition of the problem of technique and spirit in the poetry of Crashaw lies in our analysis of the epigrams and the Marinistic verse. Our solution of the problem lies in our study of the emblems and more profoundly in our study of Crashaw's intellectual and spiritual development. Chapter V, therefore, will study first the emblem and *impresa* as forms, and then the growth and illumination of Crashaw's imagery and its relation to these forms.

In these third, fourth, and fifth chapters, which involve a detailed analysis of the nature of the techniques which Crashaw studied, and of what he did with them as a purely technical problem, we can hardly avoid certain tracts very arid for the lover of poetry. But even when they are most dry, they present intellectual and critical problems of the greatest interest, and in the end we shall recapture the more fully, as the reward of our study, the "poet and saint" who so deeply impressed his own world. And while we concentrate upon the problem of techniques, and of devices of poetic style, we shall at the same time be constantly endeavoring in and through the mechanical aspects to get at the poetic spirit which informs and transmutes them. And we shall pay attention, so far as we know dates, to Crashaw's progressive development.

Even in the most arid reaches, and where the rigid techniques most fully absorb his imaginative energy, to study Crashaw's style is to come to the heart of his poetry. For in his poetry are met two strangely mingled elements, an exceptionally rich sensuous and emotional endowment, and a high degree of stylization within conventional and rigidly mechanized modes of expression. His style is deliberately fantastic, stiff with surface elaborations, overluxuriant in little detached fancies, little sensuous delights that cling radiantly but irrelevantly to the surface, in little rivulets of aesthetic refreshment, slipping north, east, south, and west from the current of the main stream. And yet no poet seeks more than Crashaw, in the end, to absorb all sense perceptions and every fragment of aesthetic experience into a single vision; and no poet strives more than he to make of them all simply the instruments wherewith the seer expresses an idea to us and evokes in us a vision. For, on the one hand, drilled as he was in conventionalized modes of expression and sensuous as he was, on the other hand, in his nature, so sensuous "that the sense faints picturing him," he yet sought to make of all the flower stems of his rhetoric, of all the sense images, the abstract and ideational counters of a vision,—the revelation of a world behind the world of the senses. And this vision is our real concern. If we study his style in detail, it is only that we may fully understand the paradox of unbridled sensousness, and unrestrained ingenuity, together aiming at abstract spirituality, which is the essence of his poetry. And the heart of that poetry lies in his transmutation of rigid forms to life.

Its outer secret lies in the story of what happened to the forms themselves; its essential energy will have been revealed to us in the story of Crashaw's life and inner growth. The mode and the spirit fuse to form his greatest poetry, and this fusion will form the subject of our closing chapter.

## Chapter II

# CRASHAW'S LIFE AND INNER GROWTH

Of Richard Crashaw's external life we know little, of his interior development there is almost no explicit record. Yet the objective facts of his history with their outline of stark drama suggest much as to the inner development if we can interpret them rightly. Our scant personal knowledge of him may at some points be extended by our knowledge of his age. What we know of the history of the time and its intellectual currents, what we know of the temper of the particular worlds in which Crashaw lived, does not, conscious as we are of the infinite varieties of the human mind, yield us any certainties as to Crashaw. Yet if we bring these sources of knowledge to bear upon the objective facts of his intellectual history, they are illuminating. The man who has been to the South Pole must have traversed the great ice fields, by whatever course he took. And the son of a noted anti-Catholic divine, who was an intimate of Little Gidding, who became fellow at Peterhouse under Cosin, and who died in Catholic orders at Loreto must have lived through a very intense religious experience. We may unite the knowledge we can gather of his life, too, with the personal revelations in his poems and with what we know of his reading. The matter of reading must indeed be handled with special precaution. Certain books, such as the principal Church fathers, we may be fairly sure that Crashaw read; at what period he read them, and at what period, or which ones, he studied intensively, we have no indication. Of certain other groups of literature, we know that they were being read by the men among whom, both spiritually and in the flesh, Crashaw lived; but which particular ones shall we say shared in that selective process by which Crashaw grew to a fruit so different from all the other men nourished in the soil of Peterhouse at that time? Even as to the books to which we are led by his poems we are in doubt; his Saint Teresa poems are clearly the immediate outcome of a fresh and intense impression of Saint Teresa; but even in the literature of St. Teresa, we are ignorant as to exactly how much of the saint's works he had read, and far more important, we do not know to what extent purely literary influences, such for instance as the emblems and sonnets of Gio. Vincenzo Imperiale, in his *La Beata Teresa,*[1] which Crashaw might have seen, tempered the direct intellectual and spiritual influence on him of the saint's life and works. In the case of other books we are more uncertain still what weight to give them in the story of his growth. The fact that he wrote on Lessius shows, indeed, that the *Hygiasticon* of Lessius interested him deeply, but his poem is an occasional poem written for the translation of Lessius about to be reissued from the Cambridge press, and we cannot measure the importance to him of Lessius relative to that of other books for which there was no such invitation to write. Then again of the *Sarum Primer,* which was the almost certain source of Crashaw's *Office of the Holy Crosse,*[2] and very probably the source in which he knew the *Stabat Mater* (which was not then in the Roman Breviary) and other of the medieval hymns; was the Primer known to him in his childhood in his father's library, as Miss White temptingly suggests,[3] long shaping his imagination with its rhythms and its color and played on for long years in turn by the other forces present in his mind; or did he come to know it amid the associations of Little Gidding, as Signor Praz surmises;[4] was it familiar to Peterhouse men as part of the Laudian enrichment under Wren and Cosin; or did he first feel it deeply as consolation amid the anguish of his uncertainty after his flight to Holland? In this period of exile, seemingly, he translated the hymns.

Bearing such limitations in mind, then, we may study the man in his life.

The record of Crashaw's life before he entered Cambridge is brief and sad. He was born in London in 1612 or 1613, the

[1] Genoa, 1615. The emblems and the epigraphs of this book are in the style which interested Crashaw. For example, a hand of Moses making a path through the sea entitled, a first miracle, and she too wrought miracles; with the epigraph: *Acta manu Hebraei Ducis admiranda patravit Virga Diu; et nostro tempore Virgo Dei.* The sonnets contain a series of reflections on the life and spirit of the saint in the following manner: You longed to show yourself to the infidel rebel.. . . A child in years and not a babe in power, you would declare yourself that of the eternal God who has Paradise you have the sun in your bosom, and the dawn in your face. This verse has the type of figure present in Crashaw's St. Teresa poems, though it is not smelted by the same ardor.

[2] See L. C. Martin, ed. Crashaw, *Poems* (Oxford: 1927) Note to p. 263, p. 447.

[3] Helen C. White, *English Devotional Literature (Prose) 1640-1660,* (Madison: 1931) p. 141.

[4] Mario Praz, *Scentismo e Marinismo in Inghilterra* (Firenze: 1925) p. 179.

son of William Crashaw, an Episcopal clergyman of some note as an anti-Catholic controversialist. At the time of the poet's birth, and for about the first six years of his life, William Crashaw was preacher at the Temple; from 1618 until 1626 he was minister of St. Mary Matfellon, Whitechapel. In that year William Crashaw died. The poet had already been deprived in early childhood, first of his mother, the date of whose death we do not know, and then of a loving stepmother, whom William had married in 1619, and who died in childbirth only seventeen months later. In 1629, some three years after his father's death, Richard Crashaw entered the Charterhouse, from which he passed to Pembroke College, Cambridge, in July 1631.

The influence of his father must have been the strongest one in his childhood and early youth. William Crashaw would seem to have been an energetic and passionate man of a somewhat clamorous type. His controversial work betokens zeal for his cause rather than a critical or philosophical temper, but there is intellectual energy in it and a genuine concern for right. This same concern led on at least one occasion to a sermon so vehement that the preacher was reported to the bishops (presumably for extreme Puritanism) at a time when men of less earnest sincerity expressed themselves more circumspectly.[5] The ague into which his "griefe & anger" threw him on that occasion, together with his anxiety not only to be dutifully serviceable to a patron but to make clear that he had been so, at the time of the death of Thomas, brother of Sir Julius Caesar, betrays a naïve egotism.[6] But these surface violences of temperament had beneath them springs of intellectual energy, of ardent feeling, and of tenderness. The tribute to his second wife instances the last quality. And in the midst of the controversial bias which marks his approach to the great tradition of his religion, we find a sensitive and ardent response to the depth and beauty of the great writers; if he could damn violently, he could also preach, "And say not, thou wast converted but thou hast forgotten it: for canst thou forget the time when thou wast married? When thy eldest son was borne? when thy ships came home, when a great and unexpected inheritance fell unto thee?

[5] Letter to Sir Robert Cotton, July 1609. Ms. Brit. Bibl. Cotton. Julius Caesar III. Letters to Sir Robert Cotton, No. 126.

[6] Letter to Sir Julius Caesar, 1610. British Museum Ms. 12479. Caesar Papers. Folio 2, recto.

Much lesse. . . ."[7] The vehemence of William Crashaw can not have been sympathetic to his son, nor can Richard have been seriously interested by the controversial approach to religion, though his early poetic exercises show him of the right anti-Roman gust. But, as Mr. Martin points out, Richard's paraphrase of Psalm xxiii shows the direct influence upon the son's imagination of the poetic strain in the father;[8] and one can imagine a sympathetic communion of mind between father and son that must have left an impression on the deepest strains of the son's nature, when William Crashaw was at work not upon controversy, but upon reading and selecting and editing the Church Fathers, and when the ardent side of his nature lay open in daily life. One of the most beautiful passages in the son's poetry, written at the height of his ardor, seems to speak of this enkindling influence of the father. In 1605 William Crashaw had edited various treatises, theological, controversial, and devotional, of M. W. Perkins, a minister then recently dead. And in the Epistle Dedicatory to *Of the Calling of the Ministerie, Two Treatises, discribing the Duties and Dignities of that Calling*, he had written,

> Had it been as well brought foorth by *me*, as it was begot by *him*, it had beene a *child* not unwoorthy of so great a *father;* . . The treatise rightly treats together of the duties and the dignities of a minister. Therefore in this *building*, these *two beames* are in great wisdome well set together by this wise *Master builder*, . . The *father* whilst he lived was a shining light in this our church, and being dead, is a shining starre in heaven, for *he turned manie to righteousness*, and his doctrine will shine, . .

And this passage, as well as Biblical phrase, may well have been in the son's memory when he wrote,

> Thou shalt looke round about, and see
> Thousands of crownd soules, throng to bee
> Themselves thy crowne, sonnes of thy vowes:
>
> . . . .
>
> Of thousand soules whose happy names,
> Heaven keeps upon thy score (thy bright
> Life, brought them first to kisse the light
> That kindled them to starres,).

[7] *A Sermon preached in London before the right honorable the Lord Lawarre, Lord Governor and Captaine Generall of Virginea and others of his Maiesties Counsell* etc. *At the said Lord Generall his leave taking . . . for Virginea.* Febr. 21, 1609. By W. Crashaw. p. 17.

[8] Crashaw, ed. Martin, *Introduction*, p. xix.

Of his schooling we know nothing that would particularize it from that of other scholars at the Charterhouse. We know that he must have studied the Bible diligently, have received an excellent grounding in Latin and Greek, have written many exercises in Greek and Latin verse that on the one hand emphasized the technical rhetorical element in expression and on the other perfected a sense of craftsmanship in poetry. Just what was the nature of these exercises we shall see in our chapter on his early verse. One can hardly imagine his deep love of music and his skill in it not to have formed one of the delights of these early years. How early his poetic genius took possession of him we do not know; the early poetic ventures of those who afterwards become poets are remembered more glowingly by their biographers than the verses of those for whom verse-writing is only a flash from generally awaking emotion.

Crashaw's intellectual and spiritual development during his later school years must have had the intensity peculiar to adolescents who stand alone. Under the English system a tremendous share of the youth's intellectual environment is, in all events, entrusted to his school; this influence is, however, constantly checked and shaped both by periods at home, and by constant threads of thought and feeling centered in the home. But Crashaw had been deprived at seven of the care of a loving stepmother, and at fourteen, before he entered Charterhouse, he had lost his father. Thus alone, he would have felt very early, as some men never feel it, the need to create for himself his own profoundest relations with life. The course of his development is in part adumbrated, but only adumbrated, in the shift of his religious views. His Gunpowder poems, which read like school-exercises, give no evidence of other than conventional religious thought—in this case anti-Catholic,—which may have expressed the prevailing temper of the school or which may have been due to his father's influence. By 1635 when, at the age of twenty-two, he was elected to his fellowship, he had developed a religious passion and high church views. Knowing as we now know his intimacy with the Ferrars at the time he took his fellowship, we wonder whether the influence of the community at Little Gidding may not have begun early in his life and may not have counted for much in this religious development.

William Crashaw had in 1609 preached a sermon to Lord Lawarre and a company setting out for Virginia and had kept up some contact with the group. And it is not impossible that in this way he may have become known to Nicholas Ferrar and his father, who were deeply concerned in the affairs of the Virginia company, and that Nicholas Ferrar, to whom the genuine piety of William Crashaw would have been sympathetic, if his controversy was not, interested himself in the son so early orphaned. If, as has been already suggested, young Richard had read widely in his father's library, there must have been much that would draw him and the older man together and would make the character and ideas of Nicholas Ferrar deeply interesting to those forces in the boy's nature which turned him away from theological question and towards personal devotion. However early the influence began, by the time Crashaw entered Peterhouse he was an intimate of the community at Little Gidding; and in the ordered life of personal devotion he fashioned for himself at Peterhouse, he sought to transplant for himself there the life of prayer and pious work established at Little Gidding in which he had shared. That community offered to him as its pattern a regular day organized primarily for the service of private and liturgical prayer; the cultivation of the arts of music, drawing and embroidery, as arts of piety; and constant devotional reading;—exercises all ministering as preparations to that personal dedication to God exemplified in Nicholas Ferrar himself. For the importance which Crashaw placed upon art as an enlargement of ritual, we remember that music, drawing, and painting all formed part of the order of his religious life at Peterhouse. It is still more significant to reflect that Crashaw, even where he expresses the most personal ecstasy, is a deliberate artist in the sense in which Spenser and Milton and Herrick are artists, and in which Herbert and Vaughan are but inspired amateurs. That profound fact in his temperament and imaginative organization both contributes to the course of his religious development and is on the other hand also a fruit of it. Besides accustoming Crashaw to a highly ritualistic practice, and to the religious concepts implied in this ritual Little Gidding was important too because certain ideas and intellectual sympathies toward which Crashaw was developing prevailed also there. The reading at Little Gidding was chosen—without disguise or purgation—for its substance, with no regard for the orthodoxy or uncleanness of its provenance. Thus the *Story Books* of Little Gidding contained among their patterns of virtue matter so varied in sources as Queen Elizabeth's words to her Parliament—"They are happiest that go hence soonest"—and the lives of Philip II and Charles V of Spain and of several of the popes. Then too the *Sarum Primer* was in use there; and such guides to ascetic and contemplative life as the Jesuit Lessius's *Rule of Health* and the *Devine Contemplations* of Juan Valdes were treasured. Though, despite popular charges of Popery levelled against Little Gidding,—as against Laudianism in general,—there is no evidence and no ground for surmise that the Ferrars ever considered a move to Rome, and though, indeed, Crashaw's letter from Holland to a member of the Ferrar family shows on the contrary a fixed barrier of thought between them and Rome, the attitude of the community toward the Roman Church and her achievements was one of respectful admiration.[9] If on Sundays during meals they read Foxe's *Book of Martyrs*, that textbook of the Established country gentry, and shibboleth of right-minded anti-Catholicism, one feels sure that they drew from it the lesson not of the infamy of the makers of the martyrs, but of the holiness of the martyrs themselves. (Indeed, at the worst, they did not escape the accusation of reading it as a cover to shield their true doctrines from righteous inquisition). Little Gidding seems to have been Arminian; it certainly believed, too, in the efficacy of works, or in the obligation to them, and had an established system of charity and instruction. Finally, at Little Gidding Crashaw made trial of the ordered quiet of withdrawal from the world into monastic life.

Nicholas Ferrar had been ordained deacon by Laud himself, and many of the prayers in use at Little Gidding were taken from the book of devotions selected by Cosin (later Master of Peterhouse) in 1627, drawing from the prayers of earlier days, so that there was nothing in the idea or in the content of the services established at Little Gidding by Nicholas Ferrar which might not have come to Crashaw through Cambridge Laudianism. But they perhaps came to him first through Little Gidding, and, what is most significant, they came to him there not primarily as a religious system, but in the form of example and personal ex-

[9] See the letter and Mr. Martin's comment on it in his edition of Crashaw, p. xxvii.

perience of an intense order. This fact would be of peculiar importance to Crashaw, whose gift was not for philosophy or the definition of doctrine or for organization, but for intense living. Of the many who subscribed to and helped to create Laudianism as a matter of doctrine and of taste in the satisfaction of their religious emotion, few indeed, like Crashaw, surrendered to the life of devotion. And it was seemingly Nicholas Ferrar who made to him the important personal communication of such a life of devotion. Little Gidding showed him, too, the power of aesthetic experience in music and drawing to minister to that life. Finally, it may well have been through Ferrar that Crashaw became acquainted with the poetry of George Herbert.

Our most important clue to Crashaw's undergraduate years at Pembroke is the fact that he came forth from them ready to enter the group of fellows of Peterhouse, then in the centre of the Laudian movement. Something of the history of the inner growth that carried him to Peterhouse is revealed in his poems. This history of interior life we shall trace as a whole presently. We must here note merely, as far as we can, his intellectual position in regard to the problems which vexed his day. He had come to believe before he left Pembroke that true religion lies in the offering of the heart and in works, and at the same time that the destruction of ritual and decoration destroys religion.[10] This latter belief is indirectly important in defining the precise meaning of the former. His attitude toward Puritanism was harshly critical. It seemed to the Puritans that Laudianism, like Catholicism, with its ritual substituted formalism for true intellectual assent and self-discipline. It seemed to the Laudian that the Puritan substituted certain formal shibboleths, outside the purlieus of religious experience, for personal devotion.

> . . . The hypocrite shall th'*upright* be
> Because he's stiffe, and will confesse no knee:[11]

By the time of Butler such an epigram against Puritan rigidity would have implied a "reasonable" high church position, firm as

[10] *On a Treatise of Charity*, Martin, pp. 137-139, and *An Epitaph Vpon Mr. Ashton*, p. 192. The poem on Mr. Ashton seems by its content to be very close in date to the poem on charity. The explicit reference in the former to doctrinal position suggests that the problem was fresh in Crashaw's mind.

On the objective evidence for the dating of Crashaw's poems, I rely upon the facts and the cogent arguments marshalled by Mr. Martin in the third section of his *Introduction*, pp. lxxxvii, and upon the valuable additions made by Mr. Austen Warren.

[11] *On a Treatise of Charity*, 11. 39-40. See also the *Epitaph Vpon Mr. Ashton*.

to church and state, and sober enough, in all truth, in its ideal of religious practise. But in the ardor and in the intellectual warfare of Crashaw's day which were driving earnest men to the extreme logic of their positions, it meant a highly ritualistic conception of religion. Apparently to the early Peterhouse years belongs also the Latin poem, *Fides quae sola justificat non est sine Spe & Dilectione*, with its strong emphasis on *Amor* as the soul in the body of *Fides*. The little poem in praise of Bishop Andrewes, *Upon Bishop* Andrewes his *Picture before his Sermons*, published in 1631, is another valuable indication of the same tendency. Crashaw had written, moreover, poems for two books by Catholic authors, the first the poem on charity just cited, written for Robert Shelford's *Five Pious and Learned Discourses* in 1635, after he had proceeded B.A., and the second that for the translation of Lessius' *Hygiasticon*, 1634. The former poem expresses, too, a distinct contempt for anti-Popery as well as for Puritanism.

The Pembroke years were very busy ones in literature. A number of translations from the classics of small pieces and fragments, such as Virgil's *Spring*, the version of *Vivamus mea Lesbia*, and some Alexandrian bits, show Crashaw moving in the ordinary undergraduate current of his day, though he hardly sought as did the ordinary undergraduate to make the lighter classics his real models. If one thinks of Cowley's *Anacreontics* and then takes a few lines of Crashaw's Catullus, one will feel the difference.

> Soles occidere et redire possunt;
> Nobis, cum semel occidit breuis lux,
> Nox est perpetua una dormienda.
>
> Brightest *Sol* that dyes to day
> Lives againe as blith to morrow,
> But if *we darke sons of sorrow*
> Set; ô then, how long a Night
> Shuts the Eyes of our short light!

The one great line reveals a passionate sense of mystery, embedded in the fantastic intellectualities of a strained rhetoric. The passion of that one line is significant for Crashaw's inner life. The rhetoric is the product of his special intellectual and artistic development. For aside from the subjects of his curriculum, Crashaw probably wrote during these years many of his Greek and Latin epigrams,[11a] and he was making also that intensive study of Marino which will be the subject of our fourth chapter. As we shall see when we study the relationship in detail, the study was not purely a stylistic one. It was the product of a restlessness not at home in either the Jonsonian classical tradition nor the classicism opened to a Milton; and not satisfied either with the great tradition of Spenser in which, nevertheless, Crashaw, like Milon, steeped himself either now or a little earlier. Other poems as well as the one quoted reveal both the Marinism and the deeper note of question overlaying the classical studies of his formal schooling. Some of his epitaphs, for instance, express the themes and concepts that belong to epitaphs in the tradition of the Anthology. But their spirit and imagery are wholly other. Crashaw brought to these exercises the spirit of the Marinistic studies which were engaging his more eager attention. To his undergraduate days belong also, in all probability, the "Marinizations" in English of his Greek and Latin epigrams. Some of these, however, which he turned into longer poems, especially *On the bleeding wounds of our crucified Lord* strike into lines that are not merely literary exercises, as,

> Thy restlesse feet they cannot goe,
> For us and our eternall good. . . .

These poems show Crashaw already attracted to a continental type of religious exercise as well as to the purely literary aspects of Marinism. A something of ecstasy in their tone, palpable amid the literary gingerbread, suggests the possibility that Crashaw was already reading attentively serious Catholic meditations on the Passion, such as he might have found, for instance, in Thomas à Kempis.

Meanwhile, one is pleased to know, he engaged lightly in the normal undergraduate inquiry into the state of his heart, but in the only poem on this theme that bears the characteristic impress of his genius and temperament, the lady is still a Divine *Idæa* that has not yet taken a shrine of Chrystall flesh.

---

[11a] See Mr. Austen Warren's "Crashaw's Epigrammata Sacra." *The Journal of English and Germanic Philology* volume 33 (1934), pp. 233-239.

Crashaw was in sympathy with the manners of the time and place, too, when he wrote occasional poems; seriously for royalty, for deaths of note to his college, playfully for the little importances of his daily world in *On a foule Morning, being then to take a journey,* and *To the Morning. Satisfaction for sleepe,* the latter of which is delightfully headed in one manuscript, *To ye Deane on occasion of sleeping chappell*; on which occasion he was only afraid of having offended Apollo!

One such occasional poem, not written, indeed, until Peterhouse days, deserves special attention because it has never before been noted and because it touches our imagination by giving Crashaw a share in the most famous of all volumes of occasional verse. *Justa Edouardo King Naufrago* contains an elegy in Latin elegiacs signed R.C. (the fourteenth set of verses), which is written in the style of verbal play and paradox thoroughly characteristic of Crashaw. King is lost, but he is not lost; he lives above. Let ships go on:

> In liquido horrentis tumulati mormore ponti
> Hoc solidum marmor nomen inane capit.
> Sed nec inane tamen: dum stat modo tempus et aether,
> Flumina dum Chami lenius ipsa meant; . . .

and so on. The probability that Crashaw should have written for this occasion is strengthened not only by the fact that so many other sons of Cambridge who were noted as poets contributed to the volume, but also by the fact that Crashaw's particular friend Joseph Beaumont was among them.

Of what friendship meant to him at this time we have no record. The number of his poems on the death of Mr. Herrys, a fellow of Pembroke, suggests that Crashaw may have had a feeling of personal loss, though he can have known Mr. Herrys for only a few months at most. Or it may only indicate, as Mr. Martin points out, that he brought with him to college a certain repute as a poet and that consequently on such an occasion he was asked or expected to write.[12] Music must certainly have been among his deep emotional satisfactions in these years. He could not have learned music so thoroughly as he knew it and as he used it at Peterhouse only after he went there; it is natural to surmise

[12] *Op. cit.*, p. xxi.

that he had studied it, as did Milton, in his childhood. But certainly, when, sometime before the end of 1635, he wrote *Musicks Duell* he was a connoisseur. The theme he took from Strada, and the endeavor to imitate pure music in verse was probably modeled on such poems as the poem of the Marinisto, Tamoso Stigliani, *La Cantatrice, a Settimia, figluola di Giulio Romano*; but the abundance of carefully used musical terms and the subtle shadings with which he tries to define various aspects of the music show great musical knowledge as well as great sensibility.

As we gather together these impressions of Crashaw's undergraduate years, we feel that his residence at Pembroke included a period of intensive literary study and of experimentation in the formation of a conscious and highly mannered style, and that it covered a far reaching change in religious ideas and sympathies from those of his father and those which were his at least formally when he wrote the Gunpowder poems. This change probably culminated in his latest undergraduate years—at least, the explicit poems to which we owe our account of it date then,—and one may surmise that it would owe something to his concentration on his formal professional studies at the same time he was going through the personal experience that is manifest in the feeling of the poems. The poem *On a Treatise of Charity* has a somewhat controversial tone and something of the simple-lined clarity of the young and newly convinced. But, despite the note of controversy, the tone of this and of the other poems on kindred themes would suggest that Crashaw's conviction had developed in a sympathetic atmosphere and without any sense of violent wrench. As Mr. Warren has shown in the article just cited, many of the epigrams were written in sequences of the religious festivals observed at Pembroke. As we saw in speaking of the influence of Ferrar and Little Gidding, actual religious exercise is likely to have preceded doctrinal concept with Crashaw, and strange as it seems to us who look back on the outcome, if the pious and poetic strains in his father had been those which the boy felt rather than the intellectual currents, he would now despite his anti-anti-Popery have had no sense of a break with his tradition, the needs of the time having so much changed. It would never have occurred to him that he was moving toward Rome.

We may assume, then, that when Crashaw entered Peterhouse the intellectual aspect of his faith was for the time being settled. It was settled on extremely high church lines. And we may well question whether, if the times had allowed him to rest in the life he created for himself there, he would have gone to the Catholic Church. He owed his conversion, according to the Queen's letter,[13] to "la Lecture et son estude." He may have had a special collection of Catholic literature from his father's library, as Miss White suggests, though this seems doubtful. But in general English devotional interest depended much on Catholic sources, both those found in earlier English books and those from earlier and contemporary continental writings, so that a wide reading in Catholic literature implied only devout preoccupation, and not a course of doctrinal instruction.[14]

Crashaw entered at Peterhouse upon a life of devotion. Laud was eager in training young men of brilliant parts for controversy; even Jeremy Taylor, whose genius seems to us so little suited to controversy, was put in training for this task. But the accounts of Crashaw would suggest that his dedication rather to a life of prayer modeled on that of Little Gidding was recognized as his vocation. His appointment as curate and catechist at Little Saint Mary's was conducive to this life. In the fulfillment of his duties there he was apparently relieved from part of his academic teaching, as we may surmise from the small number of students assigned to him as compared with those assigned to other tutors[15] so that the picture of his many hours in the chapel given in the Preface to *Steps to the Temple*, 1646, is probably not exaggerated. It was a way of life to which the Anglican Church at that time was profoundly sympathetic. The interest and admiration aroused by the community at Little Gidding, an interest in which even the king shared, and by the saintly George Herbert, were very great. And the admiration for Crashaw's own devotion aroused in so this-worldly a mind as Abraham Cow-

---

[13] Martin, p. xxxiii.

[14] The publisher of Lessius's *Hygiasticon* (It was printed by the Printer to the Universitie of Cambridge), already alluded to, apologizes for publishing two books by Catholics, one of them a Jesuit, on the ground that no harm can be taken therefrom by true Protestants. The second Catholic book in the volume was George Herbert's translation of Cornaro. For a comprehensive account of this situation, see Miss White, *op. cit.*, *passim*. An interesting special account is also given in "Catholic Writers and Elizabethan Readers" by H. Thurston, S. J., *The Month*, December 1894.

[15] See the lists given in T. A. Walker's Admission to Peterhouse or S. Peter's College in *the University of Cambridge: a biographical register*. (Cambridge: 1912)

ley's is further witness to the general sympathy toward such a course; only elsewhere in the ode to his dearest friend Hervey does the intellectual-tempered Cowley show any such feeling as he expresses in the lines to Crashaw beginning,

> Poet and Saint, to thee alone are given
> The two most sacred names of earth and heaven.

According to the letter of Henrietta Maria to the Pope, Crashaw had been educated at the Universities in England "Parmy des gens tres esloignez des sentiments de nostre Sainte Religion." But nothing in the letter suggests that she knew Crashaw or the circumstances of his life at all well and perhaps the source of her misapprehension may be found in the more explicit and correct statement of Sir Kenelm Digby in his second application on Crashaw's behalf: "Sr Ricardo Crescia (il dotto figliolo del famoso heretico dell' istesso nome)." Each side, naturally, prided itself most on those converts who had been most deeply rooted in error. Three other of the fellows of Peterhouse as well as Crashaw went to Rome.

In 1635 Crashaw, then twenty-two, was elected to his fellowship at Peterhouse. The temper of Peterhouse was particularly sympathetic to Crashaw's views. Dr. Cosin, then Master, had published in 1627 *A Collection of Priuate Deuotions*: *in the Practice of the Ancient Church, called, The Houres of Prayer. As they were much after this manner published by Authoritie of Eliza.* 1560. And in 1641 Peterhouse was to come under specially severe notice because there first Dr. Wren, who had preceded Dr. Cosin in the mastership and who had brought Cosin in to pursue his own policy, had reinstituted the Latin service, had reduced the number of sermons, and had established canonical prayer.[16] The new chapel of Peterhouse, in the ordering of which Crashaw had some part[17] was richly decorated with glass from the Low Countries, with carvings and with statuary.[18] Then too college chapels in general still used in anthems and motets the passionate and elaborate Latin church music after other church services had substituted the English music which subordinated the music to

[16] *Wren's Anatomy. Discovring His notorious pranks, and shameful wickednesse. . .* (London: 1641).
[17] See Martin, p. xxii.
[18] T. A. Walker, *Peterhouse* (London: 1906).

the words.[19] And church music was a special concern of Dr. Cosin, the library at Peterhouse still containing to this day manuscript music which he specially procured to be written for his college. In the chapel and in Little St. Mary's Crashaw spent the chief of his time, in his work as curate—Lloyd speaks of the thronged sermons on Sundays and on Holidays,—in music, in poetry, and above all in meditation and prayer. Among the original lines in Crashaw's account of a religious house from Barclay's *Argenis* are the lines,

> Obedient slumbers? that can wake & weep,
> And sing, & sigh, & work, and sleep again;

The poem was presumably written after 1646, and in the tone carried in the words *weep* and *sigh* as well as in the "long & dayly-dying life" of an earlier line, it represents a period in Crashaw's life later than the Peterhouse one; but it forms an interesting commentary on Lloyd's account of "Devotions, wherein he spent many a night, at St. *Maries* Church.[20] Lloyd speaks, too, of his diet "temperate to a Lesson exactness" and one recollects that Lessius names among the virtues of abstinence that it "Addes perspicacitie to the Wit, and clearness and aptnesse to the receiving of divine Illumination."[21] Intensive reading, too, must have engaged him much.

Despite the sympathy of his world, Crashaw's life must have been a lonely one, both from the nature of his pursuits and because, though his way was much admired, it does not seem to have been much chosen. The desolation of the letter which he was to write from Holland to one of the Ferrars is not merely that of a man who has been torn from his established life and from his country and from his livelihood, nor that of a man who meditates severing himself from his tradition, but seems like that of a man whose essential mental development has been isolated and without the sympathetic insight of intimates.[22] Yet how much, indeed,

---

[19] Cannon Fellowes, ed. *Tudor Church Music.* Introduction.

[20] *Memoires of the Lives . . . of those Noble . . . Personages, That Suffered. . . . In our late Intestine Wars, . . .* By Da: Lloyd, A.M. sometime of Oriel-Colledge in Oxon. London . . . MDCLXVIII. Cited by Mr. Martin, *Appendix II*, pp. 415-416.

[21] *Hygiasticon: or The right course of preserving Life and Health unto extream old Age: Together with soundnesse and integritie of the Senses Judgment and Memorie. Written in Latine by Leonard Lessius, And now done into English.* The third edition. (Cambridge 1636), p. 202.

[22] This is the letter already alluded to and cited by Mr. Martin, *Introduction*, pp. xxvii and following.

friendship meant to him is suggested in that very letter from Leyden: "God knows I cary about me y$^{e}$ mind and thoughts of some great landed man, and think my share in the hazards of England to be no small one. Can any man deny him that name and y$^{e}$ consequent cares of a great Rich man who is able to number to himself two reall friends." One such he numbered Joseph Beaumont, also a fellow of Peterhouse. Yet lonely as it may have been, his cannot during the years at Peterhouse have been other than a radiant life. And in the visits to Little Gidding he was sure of intimate understanding.

Upon this ordered world broke in the Civil War. Crashaw may have gone to Oxford for a time.[23] As Mr. Warren has shown he left Peterhouse probably at the end of January 1642/3.[23a] In February 1643/4 he was and had been for some time at Leyden, whither he had gone in company with a member of the Little Gidding community.[24] Under what pressure he earlier than the other fellows had left Cambridge, we do not know. Speaking of his distress at being separated from his "mother" who had come with him he says, "I confess *this last peece of my persecution* the very sorest," and he was in despair as to how things would go in England and not without fears for the church even should the King be restored to full power. At the time he wrote, however, he supposed the other fellows still in residence, though on April 8 following, Mr. Tolly, Mr. Beaumont, Mr. Pennyman, and Mr. Comyn were ejected, together with Crashaw himself, for not being resident when summoned.

Leyden was to him a desolate place, given over to materialism and to rationalism: "If I must be any thing of religious being, here I must not be. To be left thus at this Athens alone . . . my spirit will not support it. . . . To make it a meer Athens indeed they haue set up in the great church of S$^{t}$ Peter here the plaine Pagan Pallas, Cap a pee, with speare and Helmet, & Owl & all, in the place of saints at least which heretofore it seemes usurped the window. So that for me I am either not scholler enough or not Pagan enough for this place." Mr. Martin is, I think, right in interpreting the passage which follows this to mean that he

[23] For a discussion of this, see Martin, p. xxxii.

[23a] "Crashaw's Residence at Peterhouse." *The Times Literary Supplement*, November 3, 1932, p. 815.

[24] Mr. Martin's interpretation of the letter from Leyden seems to me wholly sound and I assume it as a basis in my discussion.

already meditated entering the Catholic Church. Yet he longed to return to his fellowship in peace: "I haue I assure you no desire to be absolutely and irrespectiuely rid of my beloued Patrimony in St Peter. No man then my self holds more high the humble scepter of such a little contentfull kingdom." He wished to keep travelling in order to put off the necessity of a final settlement. He felt too, since he was on the continent, a need to make of his stay something of a grand tour. "Besides I must see something euen for shame."

The next two and a half years are blank. Nor can the poetry be made to shed light on them. A good bit of the poetry of the 1646 volume may well have been written by 1642. When Queen Henrietta Maria wrote to the Pope to recommend him in September 1646 he had been over a year in Paris "Ou par le bon example de sa vie il a beaucoup edifié tous ceux qui ont conversé avec luy." He had been for at least that length of time a Catholic. Concerning other aspects of his life, our knowledge is scant. We have Wood's hearsay statements that he was in poverty and that it was Cowley who brought him to the attention of the Queen. And of one other friendship we have record in the publication of his volume of 1652, the friendship with Thomas Car or Miles Pinkney, founder and confessor of the Monastery of Canonesses of St. Augustin at Paris and active in the translation of religious works.

The remainder is the brief and familiar story. In Rome he languished for a year without notice until, then in poverty and ill-health, he was again called to the attention of the Pope by Sir Kenelm Digby and at the end of 1647 was given a place in the household of Cardinal Palotto. There, according to story, he was shocked at the lives of the other attendants; and it was to save him from their wrath following his complaint of them to the Cardinal that he was placed in the Cathedral of Loreto. In that cathedral, at all events, he was placed in April 1649, and there at the age of thirty-six or thirty-seven he died in August of the same year.[25]

The story of the last nine years is, then, one of anxiety and distress. We should like most to know whether amid its turmoils Crashaw was able to secure any of that quiet consecration to the

[25] The principal documents for Crashaw's life are given by Martin in his *Introduction*, Section I, and in Appendix II.

life of devotion which he had left in leaving Peterhouse, and whether such a life was necessary to his poetry. The only objective statement we have is the one concerning the more than year in Paris, that he had much edified people by the good example of his life.

It is perhaps worth while to make some surmise at this point as to the grouping of his poems, though we can only conjecture. His volumes were published, it will be remembered, in 1634 (Epigrams) in 1646, in 1648, and 1652, and a distinct version of the poem to the countess of Denbeigh in 1653. Most of his mature and characteristic religious poetry may well have been written in the peace of his fellowship. As Mr. Martin shows, 1637 is a likely date for the *Sospetto*; the poems *On a Treatise of Charity* and *In Praise of Lessius* date before this; and the two poems, *On a prayer booke sent to Mrs. M. R.* and *On the Assumption*, appear in a manuscript the major portion of which contains a sermon by Thom. Lenthall with a preface dated "Pemb: Hall: Cal: July: A° 1642://:" and in that manuscript the poems themselves are ascribed, the first to "R: Crashaw Coll: Petren:" the second to "Rob: Crashaw: A: Pet: Artib Magistr:" which renders it at least probable that they were composed while Crashaw was still at Peterhouse.[26] Another most important group is that which appeared first in the volume of 1648, and these, almost certainly written between 1645 and early 1648, might belong to the Paris year. The additions and alterations of the 1652 volume constitute a small but important body of Crashaw's verse. They must belong to the period after he had entered the household of Cardinal Palotto.

We turn then to the record of the poems themselves, seen against this background, for the inner history of Crashaw's growth.

As we have already suggested, the problem of his reading in relation to his growth is an exceedingly difficult one on which to say anything accurate or significant. We may simply sum up briefly a few mass impressions that take distinct form. The reading done in his school and undergraduate days certainly included the commonly read Latin and Greek authors, and of these the Latin poets so far interested him as to lead him to a few exercises. None of them seem, however, to have made any profound impres-

[26] See Mr. Martin's section on the Text and Cannon, *Introduction*, pp. xliii-lxxxi.

sion on his imagination or his style. Rather, during his undergraduate years he was much absorbed by Marino's religious verse, by some of the Catholic neo-Latin epigrammatists and elegists, and perhaps by the Marinisti. Toward the end of the Pembroke days he was particularly interested in devotional literature and in the special literature of the contemplative life. But we shall not cite special books which he is known to have read, or which he is likely to have had brought to his attention at Little Gidding, for we have too little specific knowledge and what we know is too casual a part of the whole. Some of these books, too, such as Thomas à Kempis, we must remind ourselves, are very likely to have been long familiar to him and long at work upon his imagination. Thomas à Kempis appears even in the reading recommended for school boys.[27] The remainder of his reading, other than the classics, about which he cared to write or from which we know that he drew in his writing is religious. Some of the many volumes of emblems, whose formative influence upon him we shall discuss in Chapter V, he read either at college or in Holland and France. These emblems were an important influence on the side of expression, or perhaps one might say more properly on the side of articulate voicing of his emotion. George Herbert's poems he sent to a friend as an angelic aid to prayer, and doubtless they suggested the title for *Steps to the Temple*. On the profound influence of St. Teresa we can only say that at least *In memory of the Vertuous and Learned Lady Madre de Teresa* was written before the end of 1645, though, as Mr. Austen Warren has shown, Crashaw probably first came to know her in 1638, and that her influence on him was for the remainder of his life an active and immediate one, as is shown not only by the additions to his St. Teresa poems, but by the constant presence in his poetry of the concept of the anguish of death through which one rises to vision, a concept so central in the work of St. Teresa that in view of his feeling toward her work it must have come to him from her. Of other reading in mystical literature the hymn *In the Glorious Epiphanie of Our Lord God* which was printed first in 1648, is based, as Martin shows,[28] on the Περι Μυστικης Θεολογιας of Dionysius Areopagita. Finally, the *Office of the*

---

[27] See Foster Watson, *English Grammar Schools to 1660* (Cambridge: 1900).
[28] Note to page 259, p. 447.

*Holy Crosse,* based on the *Sarum Primer,* and the poems based on the mediaeval hymns also appeared first in 1648 and hence were presumably written between 1645 and that date; this date, too, seems to be borne out by the evidence of their style. One ought, however, to argue from this not that Crashaw then first knew them, though he may have done so (he may well have known the hymns, too, as well as the office in the *Sarum Primer*) but that he was then in a state which made them peculiarly important to him.

It is at this point convenient to ask ourselves in view of the foreign influences on his thought and expression how far Crashaw's poetry is un-English. He was certainly enormously influenced by European literature. Perhaps one could say nothing more English about him. He was especially influenced by Marinism; so to some extent were William Drummond of Hawthornden, Stanley, Sherbourne, and Ayres,[29] while remaining perfectly English. We shall see, in spite of the enormous formal influence, how utterly different in final imaginative effect is Crashaw's *Sospetto* from its source. I remember hearing Professor H. B. Lathrop call to the attention of a class how different were the tales of Defoe from the Spanish picaresque literature which was their model, and he pointed out that this difference lay in the fact that Defoe, unlike his models, realized the feeling of his hero as an important circumstance in any adventure. This difference parallels in its own plane that between Crashaw and Marino. And the ardent feeling bound up within intense sensuousness which distinguishes Crashaw from Marino is central to the development which proceeded steadily in Crashaw's work. It is an individual thing, and yet broadly English. Still, certain other important foreign elements, in which the detail of style is an important consideration, remain to be considered in relation to the question of Crashaw's foreignness. These elements are found in his poetry on the Passion. Foreign influence in Crashaw is naturally more obvious than in Elizabethan and Jacobean drama. For the uniqueness of the rhetorical aspects of expression is more notable in the case

---

[29] Drummond's borrowings from Marino are listed in the notes to Mr. Kastner's edition of Drummond's poems (Edinburgh and London, 1913) and I have considered the relation of Drummond's work to his originals in an article in *The Publications of the Modern Language Association of America,* in November, 1933. The Marinism of Stanley, Sherbourne, and Ayres is discussed by Signor Mario Praz in an article in *Modern Language Review,* Vol. 20, 1925.

of a lyric poet, where the whole depends on imagery, than in narrative or dramatic poetry. But in the case of Crashaw, the themes too and the mode of treatment of them present a continental type of religious exercise in their dwelling upon the minutely human and physical aspects of the life of Christ and in the sensuousness of certain imagery owing its origin to the symbolic interpretation of the *Song of Songs*. Yet after a reader has made a wide run through the very minor religious verse from Elizabethan times on through 1660, these themes do not seem unique in Crashaw; they only seem for the first time to have been focused and fully developed by a man of genius devoting his whole life to religion and poetry. To put it in another way, the springs of much in Crashaw were continental. To turn to these springs, while rare in the particular course which English religion had taken, was not necessarily alien to large elements in the English temper; unless the whole Laudian movement is to be considered so. In the early years of the century, for instance, a detailed reflection upon the Circumcision would seem continental in its immediate origin. But by the time Robert Herrick and William Cartwright came to write their hymns for the King's choir such a theme is continental only in its remote provenance. The literalness of treatment and sensuousness found in the continental originals are intensified in Crashaw's poetry, moreover, by the fact that he is working in an unaccustomed medium, and by the specific nature of his gift of ecstasy, which we shall define in the course of this chapter. How deeply he grows also out of the heart of English verse, on the mere side of form, not to mention music, the reader with Spenser in hand will feel, though he cannot always specifically define. In thought and in mental growth, Crashaw hardly owed more to foreign influences than, let us say, Shelley owed to the classics, and he can hardly be said to have transmuted what he derived from foreign sources less than Shelley did.

Crashaw's reading shows a steadily developing interest in religious literature of an intensely devotional nature. The development of other aspects of his personality became more and more bound up with this interest and contributed to form the special character of his religious outlook.

From the beginning, poetry was for Crashaw an ecstasy in a very special sense. His description of poetry in *To the Morning. Satisfaction for sleepe* is worth noting:

> Hence 'tis my humble fancy finds no wings.
> No nimble rapture starts to Heaven and brings
> *Enthusiasticke* flames, such as can give
> Marrow to my plumpe *Genius,* make it live
> Drest in the glorious madnesse of a Muse,
> Whose feet can walke the milky way, and chuse
> Her starry Throne; whose holy heats can warme
> The Grave, and hold up an exalted arme
> To lift me from my lazy Vrne. . . .

As commentary on this one should consider also the description of the nightingale at the extreme of her endeavor in *Musicks Duell,* in a passage the portions of which I have underlined were added by Crashaw to his original.

> Her little soule is *ravisht*: and so pour'd
> *Into loose extasies that shee is plac't*
> *Above her selfe, Musicks ENTHUSIAST.*

Signor Praz in his *Secentismo e Marinismo in Inghilterra* points out that in common with all baroque aesthetic, Crashaw's poetry aims to go beyond the confines of its particular art to that universal art where all forms flow together, as for instance baroque art sought picturesque effects in architecture, plastic and musical effects in poetry.[30] This effort was closely related to Crashaw's sense of poetry as ecstasy. In the expanding intensity of his particular sense impressions, Crashaw sought to sink through them to something ampler, to an abstract capacity for intangible sensation and a sort of ideal presence of sensation. He reminds one constantly of Shelley's figures for the spirit of beauty,

> Like *memory* of music *fled*
> Like ought that for its grace may be
> Dear, and yet dearer for its *mystery*.

It is as a result of this feeling that he blends and interchanges images from the various senses as, for instance, in the *Hymn to the One Name*, or in *Musicks Duell.*

[30] Pp. 259 and following.

Of the rapture which music was to him, we have already spoken, and of the subtlety with which he describes different musical effects in *Musicks Duell.* The musician begins by *lightly skirmishing,* to which the nightingale replies with a *shrill* taste of her power in *quicke volumes of wild Notes*; he goes on with a *capring cheerefulnesse* as his arm moves now in a *long drawne dash,* now *tripps,* now *skipps and snatches*; she replies at first with an *unwrinckled* song, but goes on to point it with *tender accents* and joint it by *short diminutives,* reared in *controverting warbles.* Presently she *staggers in a warbling doubt of dallying sweetnesse . . . her slippery song.* He in the final trial dances *in lofty measures* and *anon Creeps on the soft touch of a tender tone,* closing at last in a full-mouthe diapason. He feels that in culmination,

> Those pretious mysteryes that dwell,
> In musick's ravisht soul hee dare not tell,
> But whisper to the world.

Most fully in the hymn *To the Name Above Every Name, the Name of Iesus* Crashaw describes the powers of the various instruments mingling to blend and become one with the harmony of the universe and to transmute themselves into Love.

> Wake; In the Name
> Of HIM who never sleeps, All Things that Are,
> Or, what's the same,
> Are Musicall;
> Answer my Call
> And come along;
> Help me to meditate mine Immortall Song.
> Come, yet soft ministers of sweet sad mirth,
> Bring All your household stuffe of Heaun on earth;
> O you, my Soul's most certain Wings,
> Complaining Pipes, & prattling Strings,
> Bring All the store
> Of SWEETS you haue; And murmur that you haue no more.
> Come, nere to part,
> NATURE & ART!
> Come; & come strong,
> To the conspiracy of our Spatious song.
> Bring All the Powres of Praise
> Your Prouinces of well-vnited WORLDS can raise;
> Bring All your LVTES & HARPS of HEAVN & EARTH;
> What e're cooperates to The common mirthe

> Vessels of vocall Ioyes,
> Or You, more noble Architects of Intellectuall Noise,
> Cymballs of Heau'n or Humane sphears,
> Solliciters of SOVLES or EARES;

The form of Crashaw's poems, too, is important in realizing the significance of music to him. To him, the metre was not merely an addition of pleasure (nor was it really so to Wordsworth) but one of the basic sensuous experiences through which he sought to penetrate to rapture. His *Sospetto d' Herode* has a Spenserian richness of music. His later lyrics are elaborate and sustained musical compositions of some two hundred and fifty lines each with which nothing can be compared except the musical periods of *Paradise Lost,* such a poem as Vaughan's *Waterfall* (which, however, is a much simpler melody, and loses its initial musical impulse before the end) and Wordsworth's *Ode on Intimations,* which owes so much to Crashaw and to *The Waterfall.* Anyone who will read aloud, for example, the hymns *To the Name Above Every Name,* and *In the Gloriovs Epiphanie,* will feel that each is as much a single and organic musical design as is a movement of a symphony. Mr. Martin suggests that in the forms of Crashaw's volume of 1648 "(particularly in the Odes) it is perhaps not too fanciful to see the influence of Cowley's liking for the 'Pindarique' form."[31] Some influence there may have been; but Crashaw already had the irregular form well in hand in the poems *On a prayer booke* and *On the Assumption,* poems which preceded Cowley's Pindariques; and the irregularity of Cowley's Pindariques has nothing of that organic structure or lyric sweep which we feel in Crashaw. This last is a subjective judgment. But I think an examination of certain relevant considerations as to contemporary forms will show that Crashaw owed his music to the direct and immediate influence of instrumental music, that it was written to "tunes," though I have not succeeded in finding any particular tune to which anything was written, and indeed there is no unlikelihood in his having composed his own. In truth one ought rather to say that he transferred the characteristic qualities of instrumental music to the different medium of verse. Professor Felix Schelling, himself a trained musician, constantly points out to his classes the direct influence of music in shaping

[31] *Introduction,* p. xxxiv.

the Elizabethan lyric forms such as the madrigal and the air; in the case of Crashaw, the metrical forms derived from the more elaborate church music of the day.

To begin with, in the *Hymne of the Nativity,* the rising musical excitement of the Full Chorus is notable. The metre throughout the hymn is iambic pentameter, freely handled with occasional initial inversion and trochaic line, or initial truncation, as it is unsatisfactorily called. [32] In the first stanza of the Full Chorus, this basic pattern is strikingly varied, the variations separating out certain melodic elements or phrases which are repeated.

```
' x x '    x ` x '
x ' x `    s' x x s'
' x x ' x    ' x '
' x x '    x ' x '
` ' x '    x ' x '  x '          ` ' x '   ` ' x '
```

Thus within the iambic melody of the basic pattern is a recurrent cretic-choriambic phrase.[33]

Very much more elaborate is the hymn *To the Name Above Every Name,* which is typical of the later lyric metres. It is accordingly worth while to scan a good portion of it. It must be noted at the outset, however, that no system of notation will give more than a skeleton of the tune. In verse music such as Waller's and the standard closed couplet, where "smoothness" was much sought, and beat and syllabization pretty much evened out, a marking of stresses and alliterations will represent the pattern fairly well. But in such verse as Crashaw's or Milton's, where the variation in syllabization is great and the presence of many polysyllables and compounds varies both stress and the imponderable element of length most subtly, and where the presence of de-

---

[32] Stanza 2 runs thus (version of 1648.) (Stanza one is introductory and is irregular in being only four lines).

```
' x ' x ' x '          ' xx ' x ' x '
' x ' x ' x '          ' x ' x ' x '
' x ` x ' x '
' x ` x ' x '
```

[33]

Wellcome, all WONDERS in one sight!
  Aeternity shutt in a span.
Sommer in Winter. Day in Night
  Heauen in earth, & GOD in MAN.
Great little one! whose all-embracing birth
Lifts earth to heauen, stoopes heau'n to earth.
(Text of 1648)

The reader will note the alliteration which marks the first phrase; the fact that in the third line the first phrase is not a perfect choriambic but is so in effect, as the last syllable almost disappears; and the fact that "&" in the fourth line is so little voiced as to be almost pure rest, and the alteration of the choriambic to a new but kindred pattern in the last two lines. I use the Greek terms as being convenient and customary descriptions, *not as representing any structural intention.* I have used ' to mark a heavy stress; ` for a secondary stress.

liberate vowel-slides creates subtle ligatures that further enrich what we may call the "pitch" of the notes as distinct from their "time" (using the parallel of instrumental music), the notation represents something much less than the tune. To take only one instance, it is clear that the main stresses of any given line are not actually equal, sometimes not nearly so, but that what constitutes the pattern is the *proportional relation* (in part influenced by length) of the stressed to the unstressed syllables with which they unite to form a group or foot, and that this proportional relation is fairly constant. But in such "regularized" lines as Waller's the stresses must be nearly equal, whereas in Milton and Crashaw, the repetition in the constitution of the foot, combined with this variation in what we may call the mass of the foot adds a new element (besides the explicit variations from the formal pattern) to that play of secondary melodies against basic line pattern which is of the essence of all great verse.[34] This, particularly if skilfully used, parallels "accent" in music.

Professor William Ellery Leonard has raised with me the issue whether in the following scansion in marking variations of accent from the "normal" or "regular" pattern I have not confused "pitch-stress" with "metrical accent." I have considered this very carefully in the light of various recent investigations and theories of verse as well as of my own interpretation of what I hear in the total structure of Crashaw's verse and in other verse compared with it. Bearing in mind the imponderables I have named above, and that are not represented by the notations, I believe (though I hesitate to disagree with such an authority) that the metrical accents fall as I have indicated. With these necessary limitations of notation in mind, then, we may scan a passage from the hymn.

1. I *S*ing the *N*AME which *N*one can say — 4 a
   (accents: ′ ′ ′ ′; below: 1 1)

2. But *t*ouch't with An in*t*eriour RAY: — 4 a
   (accents: ′ ‵ ′ ′)

3. The *N*ame of our *N*ew PEACE; our Good: — 4 b
   (accents: ′ ‵ ′ ′; below: 1 1)

---

[34] See Paull F. Baum, *The Principles of English Versification*, (Cambridge: 1922) for interesting general definitions.

´ ` ´ ´
4. Our *B*lisse: & Supernaturall *B*lood: 4 b

´ ´ ´ ´
5. The *N*ame of All our *L*iues & *L*oues. 4 c
1

´ ´ ´ ´
6. *H*earken, and *H*elp, ye *h*oly Doues! 4 c
2 2 2

´ ` ´ ´ ´
7. The *h*igh-born *B*rood of Day; you *b*right 4 d
2 3 3

´ ` ´ ´
8. Candidates of *b*lissefull *L*ight 4 d
3 1

´ ´ ´ ´ ´
9. The HEIRS elect of *L*oue; whose Names belong 5 e
4

` ´ ´ ´ ´
10. Vnto The euer*l*asting *l*ife of *S*ong 5 e
4 4 5

` ` ´ ` ´ ´
11. All ye wise *S*OVLES, who in the wealthy *B*rest 5 f
5 5

´ ´ ´ ´ ´
12. Of This vnbounded *N*AME *b*uild your warm *N*est. 5 f
6 6

´ ´ ´ ´ ´
13. A*w*ake, My glory. *S*OVL, (if such thou be, 5 g
7

` ` ´ ´ ´ ´
14. And That *f*air *W*ORD at all re*f*eer to Thee) 5 g
7

´ ´
15. A*w*ake & Sing 2 h
7

` ´
16. And be All *W*ing; 2 h
7

´ ´ ´ ´ ´
17. Bring *h*ither thy *w*hole *S*ELF; & let me *s*ee 5 g
8 8

´ ´ ´ ´
18. What of thy Parent *H*EAVN yet speakes in thee. 5 g
8

´ ´
19. O thou art *P*oore 2 i
9

´ ´ ´
20. Of *n*oble *P*OWRES, I see, 3 g
10 9

´ ´ ´ ´ ´
21. And full of *n*othing *e*lse but *e*mpty ME, 5 g
10

´ ´ ´ ` ´
22. *N*arrow, & *l*ow, & infinitely *l*esse 5 j
10

` ` ´ ´ ´ `
23. Then this GREAT *m*ornings *m*ighty Busy*n*es. 5 j
10

´ ´ ´
24. One little WORLD or two 3 k
´ ´ ´

´ ´ ´
25. (Alas) will neuer doe. 3 k
´ ´

26. We must haue *s*tore. 2 l
11

´ ` ´ ´ ´
27. *G*oe, *S*OVL out of thy *S*elf, & *s*eek for More. 5 l
12 11 11 11

´ ´
28. *G*oe & request 2 m
12

` ´ ´ ` ` ´
29. *G*reat NATVRE for the KEY of her *h*uge *C*hest 5 m
12 13 13

´ ´ ´ ´ ´
30. Of *H*eauns, the *s*elf inuoluing *S*ett of *S*phears 5 n
13 13

´ ´ ` ´ ´
31. (Which dull *m*ortality *m*ore Feeles than *h*eares) 5 n
13

´ ´
32. Then *r*ouse the *n*est 2 m
14 15

´ ´ ´ ´
33. Of *n*imble ART, & trauerse *r*ound 4 o
15 14

´ ´ ´ ´ ´
34. The Aiery *S*hop of *s*oul-appeasing *S*ound: 5 o
16 16 16

´ ´ ` ´
35. And beat a *s*ummons in the *S*ame 4 p
16 16

´ ´
36. All-*s*oueraign Name — 2 p
16

´ ´ ´
37. To *w*arn each *s*euerall kind — 3 q
17 16

´ ´ ´ ´
38. And *sh*ape of *s*weetness, Be they such — 4 r
16 16

´ ´ ´
39. As *s*igh with *s*upple *w*ind — 3 q
16 16 17

´ ´ ´
40. Or *a*nswer *A*rtfull Touch, — 3 r
16 18

´ ´ ´ ´
41. That they *c*onuene & *c*ome *a*way — 4 s
17

´ ` ´ ´
42. To *w*ait at the *l*oue-crowned *D*oores of — 4 t
17 91 20

´ ´ ´
43. This I*ll*ustrious *D*AY. — 3 s
19 20

´ ´ ´ ´ ´
44. Shall we dare This, my Soul? we'l doe't and bring — 5 u
20 20

´ ´ ´ ´
45. No Other *n*ote for't, but the *N*ame we sing — 5 u

´ ´
46. Wake *L*UTE & HARP — 2 v
19

´ ´ ` ´
47. And euery sweet-*l*ipp't Thing — 3 u
19

´ ´ ´
48. That *t*alkes with *t*unefull *s*tring; — 3 u
21

´ ´ ´ ´
49. *S*tart into *l*ife, And *l*eap with me — 4 w
21

` ´ ´ ` ´ ´
50. Into a *h*asty Fitt-tuned *H*armony — 5 w

´ ´ ´
51. Nor *m*ust you think it *m*uch — 3 x

´ ´ ´
52. T'o*b*ey my *b*older touch; — 3 x

53. I haue Authority in *L*OVE'S name to take you 5y
22

54. And to the *w*orke of *L*oue this morning *w*ake you 5y
23 22 23

55. *W*ake: In the Name 2 z
23

56. Of HIM who neuer sleeps, All Things that Are, 5aa

57. Or, what's the same, 2 z

58. Are Musi*c*all; 2 bb
24

59. Answer my *C*all 2 bb
24

60. And *c*ome along; 2 cc
24

61. Help me to *m*editate *m*ine Im*m*ortall *S*ong. 5cc
25 25 25 26

62. Come, ye *s*oft *m*ini*s*ters of *s*weet *s*ad *m*irth 5 dd
26 25 26 26 25

63. Bring All your *h*ous*h*old *st*uffe of *H*eaun on earth; 5 dd
26

64. O you, my *S*oul's most *c*ertain Wings, 4 ee
26 26

65. Com*p*laining *P*ipes, and *p*rattling *St*rings, 4 ee
26

66. Bring All the *st*ore 2 ff
26

67. Of *S*WEETS you haue; And *m*ur*m*ur that you haue no *m*ore. 6 ff
26

68. Come, *n*ere to part 2 gg
27

69. *N*ATVRE & ART! 2 gg
27

70. *C*ome; and *c*ome *st*rong, 2 hh
28

71. To the con*sp*iracy of our *Sp*atious *s*ong. 5 hh[35]
28 28 28

Before pointing out the notable characteristics of this verse, we may remind ourselves briefly of the special elements in church music which might have influenced it.[36] Three points deserve mention. First, the handling of time was more varied and more free than in later music. That music was unbarred, and changed time with great freedom, and this freedom was extended by the fact that the relation of whole note (breve), half note (semibreve) and quarter note (minim) to each other was unfixed and admitted of several adjustments; in a given passage, the time might be two half notes to a whole note, or three, and again, two quarter notes to a half note, or three,—in all, four possible adjustments, offering very different effects; the possibility of variety was, moreover, extended still further by the fact that a change in this adjustment might be introduced for a single bar or part of a bar,—for instance, in a passage with two half notes to the whole note, and two quarter notes to the half note, the first voice might change and run three quarter notes to the half note for a bar, the second voice might make the same adjustment for half the bar, and one of the other voices might make it for a lesser fraction of the bar. The result of these variations is effects of beautiful contrast between very massive slow passages with massed accents, and other rapid and open passages. Then, a second point, there was more variety in the phrase length. For instance, in Orlando Gibbon's Anthem, *Glorious and Powerful God,* there is a passage in which the chorus develops in a double phrase of sixteen bars (when barred in modern notation), divided five plus five and three plus three, as against the eight bar phrases in the declamatory passage. Thirdly, the music was polyphonic.

---

[35] I have used ′ for heavy stresses; ‵ for secondary stresses; I have italicized alliterations and in addition numbered alliterations between lines.

[36] My account of the technical basis of the time in this music is a very simple one, and I would stress rather the effect of the time, which I have heard with extreme delight during performances at the Temple Church and at Westminister Cathedral. For a full statement as to the basis of time, see Cannon Fellowes' introduction to *Tudor Church Music.*

Now if we return to Crashaw's poem, points which deserve special note are, first, in the general structure of the passage, the varied line-lengths, together with the varied rhyme patterns; and the alliterations. First, in the line-lengths, the general design is to group by rhyme units composed of different numbers of lines of the same length, though this grouping is varied, as we shall see in examining the rhyme in detail. The rhyme grouping, to take up our second element of general design, is prevailingly couplet, but this couplet effect is given abundant variation, first, by rhymed lines of different length in couplets or in alternates, as 20-21; 26-27; 28-29; 35-36; 37-39; 38-40; 41-43 with a blank line between; then by occasional widely separated rhymes and triplets, as, 19-26-27, and 28-29-32; thirdly, by several groups of quatrains, *abab,* and (but these are outside our lines, 111-114 and 121-124) of quatrains *abba,* 4224; finally, it is varied by a number of blank lines enclosed within rhymes, 42, 46, 56. These variations seem to me to reproduce in their own medium musical effects of varied phrase and varied melody length.[37] In the third element of the general design, alliteration, the notable point is not the extraordinary number of alliterations, but the alliterations which cross from line to line and in so doing suggest entirely new line patterns playing across the basic line patterns. This is one of the elements which contributes most strongly to produce a polyphonic effect, especially as it combines with certain stress variations.

In stress, a number of individual variations deserve comment. Trochaic inversion in the first place is fairly common, especially in the short lines, where it creates a very definitely marked-out and stacatto phrase, ´ x x ´ which for convenience we might call choriambic, remembering always that we use the term only as it has been rendered by usage a convenient term of description, and not to indicate its structural origin. These stacatto phrases, building up to a single effect as they recur through the poem, join notably with alliteration in producing a polyphonic effect. Lines 11 and 12 have trochaic inversion within the line, and 11 and 56 spondees, one in the second and one in the fourth foot, creating clustered stresses. Clustered stresses are created, too, in lines 3, 11, 14, 16, 17, 29, 42, 44, 53, by what, if we are counting the lines

[37] In the hymn *In the glorious Epiphanie,* which is divided into different parts for the three kings and for a chorus, the correspondence to musical effects is perhaps even more striking.

as composed of iambic feet, we might call suspended stress in a double foot or bar. But the effect is distinctly that of line units with changes of time, rather than of anything that could be suggested by a nomenclature of variations in the foot. Lines 22 and 23 are interesting together, the first being decidedly light of beat and rapid, the second heavily marked and slow; in the first the unstressed syllable of "narrow" is very light and the third syllable of "infinitely" is very lightly stressed; in the next line "great" takes an extra stress and "mornings mighty" has a very heavy roll. Line 29, again, clusters the beats in the spondees of "Great NATVRE" and "her huge Chest" and drops the beat on "for." Altogether the gathering up of mass in lines 61-67 is remarkable, ending with the Alexandrine of the last line. Not only is the weight of beats in this group of lines notable, but the especially frequent alliterations both within the line and from line to line fall with extraordinary effect upon the ear:

61. h. . .m. . .m. . .m. . .s
62. s. . .m. . .s. . .s. . .m
63. h. . .h. . .s. . .h
64. s. . .s
65. pl. . .p. . .pr. . .str
66. s
67. s. . .h. . .m. . .m. . .h. . m

And, finally, lines 42 and 43 together are remarkable, for Crashaw has made 42 one of the few feminine lines (and it is a blank line) ending with a preposition, in order to stress sharply the bold phrase of the next line, which is trochaic (one of only two trochaic lines in the whole passage); and he further marks out this line by the sound concentration,—"This illustrious." The effect secured in such passages is almost like the accentuation in symphonic or ensemble music of a melodic phrase by the coming in of another instrument, or by imitation in counterpoint.

When we remember how skilled a musician Crashaw was, and how constantly he had music in his ears and in his imagination, and how little pattern for such verse he had before him in English poetry, these effects, the free handling of the basic line pattern, especially in clustered beats, the interplay of long and short melodies through freely varied line length,—especially in the marking out of the short lines by choriambic effects—and through rhyme, and the cross-line alliterations with their constant suggestions of secondary line patterns;—these effects, taken together, seem like the reproduction, in a different medium, of definite musical forms.

The probability that music directly influenced Crashaw is strengthened by other verse of the period which seems also to bear the impress of religious music. The elements we have been describing are all present, in greater or lesser degree, in a group of poems written for performance by King Charles' Choir at the great religious festivals, poems written by Robert Herrick, William Cartwright, and Martin Lluelyn, a friend and fellow student of Cartwright's; and these elements are not present in their other verse. In the case of Herrick, the reader might well compare the choral songs with the *Nuptiall Song or Epithalamie, on Sir Clipseby Crew and his Lady,* which is also an elaborate structure in varied line length but which is utterly different in structure and effect from the chorales, and is obviously, it seems to me, Greek in origin. The chorals are free in their variation; the Epithalamie, stanzaic and exceedingly formal both in the maintenance of stresses and in design. It runs in iambics 5, 5, 4, 4, 2, 5, 4, 5, 3, 4, rhymed in couplets. The seventh line is remarkable for a rest, running thus, ' x ' x ' x ' , which is exactly repeated in all of the sixteen stanzas except the twelfth, thirteenth and fourteenth, where it comes before the last beat instead of before the first. Stanzas one and two are notable for the successful division of a word between lines, in the Greek fashion. Altogether it is one of the great achievements in English verse, but in a mode very different from the chorales. Then, too, Milton's *At a Solemn Musick,* which was certainly written under the influence of religious music, is distinguished by just these effects we have noted in Crashaw of clustered heavy beat and of varied phrase length.

Whether or not the metre of these poems is to be referred to music, they are great and original verse. And in their form, they both illustrate the effect of musical ecstasy in Crashaw, and themselves, as musical compositions, express and recreate in us one of the great aspects of his passion.

As he developed, the experiences of musical and of poetic ecstasy came to identify themselves with religious ecstasy.

Crashaw's most detailed effort to give an account of his religious ecstasy is that in the poem *On a prayer booke sent to Mrs. M.R.* As we have seen, he had by 1635 come to a high-church position and had surrendered himself to the life of devotion. For him as for Herbert the division was very sharp and clear-cut between the life of the world and the religious life. The images which value the world at nothing are abundant in the literature of the period; but in Crashaw they have an intensity which reveals how literal their meaning was to him. The poem on Lessius sounds the theme, and it is vividly defined in the *Hymne of the Nativity*

> Welcome, (though not to those gay flyes
> Guilded i'th' Beames of Earthly Kings
> Slippery soules in smiling eyes)
> But to poore Shepheards, simple things,
> That use no varnish, no oyl'd Arts,
> But lift clean hands full of cleare hearts.
> (Version of 1646)

*On a prayer booke* expands the theme in the same images as this passage and intimates the life of prayer through which one may evade "false perhaps as fair, flattering but forswearing eyes." In the volume of 1648 this poem is followed by a second poem urging the young gentlewoman not merely to seek to spiritualize her life, but to renounce the world entirely, that world which is a "lower sphear of froth and bubbles" and in which she will find but "painted shapes, Peacocks and Apes, illustrious flyes, guilded dunghills . . . oathes of water, words of wind"; she is to regard her misfortune in love only as an art of Christ to "Strike your troubled heart / home to himself." So, too, in answer to Cowley's man of the world whom Hope leads astray on will o' the wisp desires, Crashaw finds in Hope an aspiration toward the divine.

> Her keele cuts not the waves, where our winds stirre,
> And *Fates* whole Lottery is one blanke to her
> (Version of 1646)

The image of man as dust, as the "dark son of dust and sorrow," is common in Crashaw, and no image is more frequently repeated than those of contrasting day and night, darkness and light. These images are common also to Vaughan. But Vaughan found his vision in the midst of an active life where it seems clear that Crashaw could never have found this.

The world once turned from, the vision which he sought he sought through pure intensity of emotion. We have already spoken of the ecstasy of poetry and music. Charity, in *On a Treatise of Charity*, is valued as a sacrifice enkindling the heart. And it is significant that, whereas for Cowley, in the Hope poems, love of woman will betray us because woman is so fickle and coquettish, for Crashaw love will delude because

> . . Loue's more feirce, more fruitless, fires assay
> One face more fugitiue then all they.

In the poem on prayer, he seeks to intimate a rapture which transcends sensation and even conscious emotion (luminous trances; soft exhalations of soul, dear and divine annihilations); yet he uses sense images to convey his experience not only here but constantly. The actual account of the vision (lines 60-86) owes much to the *Song of Songs,* but the more elaborate and specific sense imagery and sense symbolism is distinctively Crashaw's.[38] In the first version of the *Hymne of the Nativity*, much purely sensuous imagery and picture, not turned to symbol, is used to express the significance of the gift. In the opening of the poem on prayer he suggests a very concrete vision of Heaven and in the lines added to the poem *In the Glorious Assvmption* in the second version he greatly increases the sensuousness (based here on the *Song of Songs*).

Thus these earlier poems confirm the objective picture we have formed of Crashaw's life at Peterhouse and of the large part which sensuous rapture played in his life there. That rapture had been his before his devotion. As he sought to fill it with larger content, it was in terms of the same sensations, but with their new associations gathered around them to make them less and less actual, more and more symbolic. Perhaps, as we shall see

[38] "Perfume," for instance, is one of the sense elements used again and again. Thus, at the birth of Christ, "The North forgot his fierce intent and left perfumes instead of scarres": in the poem on Herbert's *Temple*, prayer is "perfumed"; and in the hymn *To the Name Above Every Name*, it is in a long description of perfumes that he entreats the divine spirit to fill him with an ideal emotion that shall shut out all sensuous impressions. (lines 165-188). Although Crashaw's symbolism is of a very distinctive type, it is interesting to remember that the figures of the *Song of Songs* too are of a symbolic character. Mr. Israel Baroway of New York University pointed out the influence of these symbolic figures, as distinct from Petrarchism, on Spenser, in a paper on "Spenser and the 'Song of Songs'," read before the Modern Language Association at their annual meeting in 1933.

in defining his imagery, his conversion to Catholicism, with the symbolism of the Mass, was important in this direction.

There is a steady pruning of the purely sensuous elements. In the 1648 version of the *Hymne in the Holy Nativity* the most luxurious and purely sensuous stanza of the first version is omitted, others are purified to something more symbolic and the great stanzas which transmute the whole are added.[39]

> Poor WORLD (said I.) what wilt thou doe
> To entertain this starry STRANGER?
>
> ................................
>
> Proud world, said I; cease your contest
> And let the MIGHTY BABE alone.
> The Phænix builds the Phænix' nest.
> Love's architecture is his own.
> The BABE whose embraves this morn,
> Made his own bed e're he was born.

The St. Teresa poems have no purely sensuous imagery and none that is merely physically ingenious except in the two lines, "teares shall take comfort, & turne gemms / And Wrongs repent to Diademms." Among the parts added by Crashaw in his *Description of a Religious House* from Barclay are the lines dwelling upon peace and obedience.[40] And the hymn *To the Name Above Every Name* pleads to be released from aesthetic to contemplative vision won through meditation on Christ.

The works of St. Teresa exerted a very profound influence in deepening the content of Crashaw's experience. As Mr. Warren has shown, he probably began his reading of St. Teresa as

---

[39]

Version of 1646

I saw th' officious Angels bring,
The downe that their soft brests did strow,
For well they now can spare their wings,
When Heaven it selfe lyes here below.
Faire Youth (said I) be not too rough,
Thy downe though soft's not soft enough

The Babe no sooner 'gan to seeke,
Where to lay his lovely head,
But streight his eyes advis'd his Cheeke,
'Twixt Mothers Brests to goe to bed.
Sweet choise (said I) no way but so,
Not to lye cold, yet sleepe in snow.

Version of 1648

I saw the obsequious SERAPHIMS
Their rosy fleece of fire bestow.
For well they now can spare their wings
Since HEAVEN itself lyes here below
Well done, said I: but are you sure
Your down so warm, will pass for pure?

NO, no, your KING'S not yet to seeke
Where to repose his Royall HEAD
See, see, how soon his new-bloom'd CHEEK
Twixt's mother's breasts is gone to bed.
Sweet choise, said we! no way but so
Not to ly cold, yet sleep in snow.

The first version, in its sensuous imagery and ingenuity seems close to the *Sospetto* (probably 1637); and the very close resemblance between the descriptions of the slippery world in this hymn and in *On a Prayer booke* suggest that the date of composition of these two is close.

[40] See Barclay, *Argenis*, book V. Crashaw's poem is based not merely on the verse of Barclay, but on the whole context.

early as 1638[41]. Only the two St. Teresa poems among all the poems which appeared in the volume of 1646 have the severer notes which color the later volumes. Before the second and third St. Teresa poems were written, Crashaw had entered the Catholic Church. Of what he felt in taking that step he tells us nothing. Looking back upon it afterward he felt only the sorrow of his delay. The poem to the Countess of Denbigh in part echoes his letter from Leyden, and it would not seem fanciful to read in it his own experience.

> What magick bolts, what mystick Barres
> Maintain the will in these strange warres!
>
> ................................
>
> 'Tis cowardise that keeps this feild
> And want of courage not to yield.

In the Saint Teresa poems and in the poems after the volume of 1646 are certain notes not found earlier. They relate Crashaw more deeply than do the previous poems to the mediaeval tradition, and to that tradition as it was carried forward in the renewed religious impulse of the Counter-Reformation, in such a life as St. Teresa's. Chief among these new notes is that of self-abasement and the desire to "wound" the heart till it is all transmuted. The earlier poetry had expressed states of joyous excitement and ardor, but had not related the ardor to the whole life of the personality. *On a prayer booke,* indeed, had dwelt briefly on the anguish of the effort to give over the world; the prayer book will fortify the hold of the heart against the world. . . .

> Dear soule bee strong,
> Mercy will come ere long, . . .
> To make immortall dressings

But this deeper note was rare. The first of the poems to St. Teresa describes with sympathetic participation the anguish of her many "deaths" which she undergoes in her struggle to subdue her whole self to her vision. The early poems on the Passion seem to me superficial exercises of the ingenious fancy; the *Stabat Mater* and *Vexilla Regis* on the other hand are written after concentrated meditation upon the Passion. Throughout this later

[41] "Crashaw and St. Teresa." *The Times Literary Supplement,* Augustus 25, 1932, p 593.

poetry the theme of the hardness and coldness of his heart, and the suffering meditation that with grace may soften it, is voiced seriously and with immediacy. Coupled with it is the image of the flame or light of ecstasy which lifts him from his vileness and from his despair. Of this theme the simplest and greatest expression is that in the last lines of *The Flaming Heart,* added after 1648. Among the passages, too, which Crashaw added to his original in the *Description of a Religious House* are the last two of the following three lines,

> A hasty Portion of praescribed sleep;
> Obedient Slumbers? that can wake & weep,
> And sing, and sigh, & work, and sleep again.

The later poems reveal not only the general concentration of Crashaw's personality, but the specific direction of his thought. Among the themes of contemplation of which he treats in this group of poems are the abasement of man (in *Charitas Nimia*), and external nature viewed as the symbolic alphabet of God (in the theme of the hymn *To the Name* and in the Epiphany hymn, in the poem to the Countess of Denbigh, and in *For Hope*[42]). The hymn *To the Name* also contemplates martyrdom with longing. The Epiphany hymn, though utterly different in its emblematic imagery and in its intellectual statement from the *Περι Μυστικης Θεολογιας* on which it is based, expresses at least the vision of surrendering the senses and their ecstasy and the ratiocinative powers in order that he may pass beyond sense-sprung perception (with some "loss of brain") to pure intuition. And the hymn *To the One Name* would subordinate and dissolve sensuous emotion in the contemplation of the ideal.

At the close of this study of Crashaw's development, finally, we may further define what was to him the relation of the sensu-

---

[42]

> Love, that lends haste to heaviest things,
> In you alone hath lost his wings.
> Look round and reade the World's wide face,
> The field of Nature or of Grace;
> Where can you fix, to find Excuse
> Or Pattern for the Pace you use?
> Mark with what Faith Fruits answer Flowers,
> And know the Call of Heav'n's kind showers:
> Each mindfull Plant hasts to make good
> The hope and promise of his Bud.

*Against Irresolution and Delay in matters of RELIGION* (1653)

> True *Hope's* a glorious Huntresse, and her chase
> The God of Nature in the field of Grace

On *Hope* (Version of 1646)

ous and the ideal by gathering together the passages in which he uses the term *intellectual*. It is found early in the poem on Lessius (by 1635) "A soule whose intellectuall beames / no mistes doe maske" The other uses are later. "Vessells of vocall Ioyes, / Or You, more noble Architects of Intellectuall Noise" (*To the Name*); "Home to the originall sourse of LIGHT & intellectuall Day," (*A Religious House*); "& presse on for the pure intelligentiall Prey"; (*Epiphanie*); "By thy larg draughts of intellectuall day," (*The Flaming Heart,* 1652).

In the first of these uses, the poet signifies clarity of thought and feeling in general; in the second, the "unheard melodies" of Keats, the ideal emotion won when musical ecstasy rises and unites with the concept of the divine in a union of meditation and aesthetic experience; in the Epiphany hymn he denotes the intuition of God which is beyond any vision that can be sensuously symbolized; and in the *Description of a Religious House* and the *Flaming Heart* the ἀνομάτους νόας or "invisibles intellectus" of Dionysius. We feel in the last group of poems an ecstasy rooted in profounder meditation than the esctasy of the earlier poems. It is still made articulate through the original sensuous ecstasy, but this is now abstracted and generalized.

Thus the history of Crashaw's inner life as he reveals it in his poetry confirms and interprets the outward movement and the intellectual history. He brought to the mediaeval religious thought toward which he finally turned all the emotional sophistications and all the sophistications of thought concept in which from the beginning he had become accustomed to embody his intellectual and his poetic ardor. But in the last years he sought to abstract from these individual patterns of emotional and intellectual life all memory of particular experience and, under the inspiration of St. Teresa, "Vnto all life of mine [to] dy." It is the energy of this emotional and spiritual development which at last transmutes to poetry the grotesque artifice of his thought and writing, and it is accordingly in the light of this development that we shall understand his style.

## CHAPTER III

# SCHOOL-WORK: THE LATIN EPIGRAM AND THE PATTERN OF THE RHETORICS

Crashaw's epigrams and the formal rhetoric which is so bound up with them are the subject of this chapter.

To define any specific influence in Crashaw's work is not easy. For the many influences are blended and superimposed upon each other in a synthesis, at various stages, and we have few actual dates to go upon. We know, for instance, that a large body of Latin and Greek epigrams and some English ones, often translations of the former, constitute Crashaw's earliest work. But in the epigrams as they are published, there are, among some which seem almost surely to have been school exercises, a very large number which Mr. Warren has shown to be written during Crashaw's three years at Pembroke and still others which are certainly translations from Marino and which, hence, were also written in Crashaw's undergraduate days. Or *The Weeper* well illustrates the complexity of the problem. That poem is one which, as we reflect casually upon Crashaw's poetry, we think of as a notable example of Marinism. In fact, however, the principal source for the poem is an epigram of the Jesuit Franciscus Remondus; but besides this, there are analogues in an epigram of Bauduinus Cabilliavus and in Hugo's *Pia Desideria*, a further source for one line in a stanza of Marino's *La Maddelena ai piedi di Christo*, and important analogues for the general theme in other of Marino's poems on the Magdalen.[1] Thus the "Marinism" of that characteristic poem rests only in small measure directly upon Marino, though the diffused and general influence upon it of the Italian poet is large. Nor does our only problem lie in the synthesis of the two influences in Crashaw. For the two groups whose impulse lies behind his poem, Marino and the Jesuit epigrammatists, though they are sig-

[1] Any one working in this field is immeasurably indebted to the extensive and minute work of Mr. L. C. Martin in his edition of Crashaw's *Poems* (Oxford: 1927). Other source work is only gleaning after him.

nificantly different in spirit, have also much in common. They spring in part from the same artistic impulse. The work of both is baroque; it is, in part, that is to say, an expression of that widespread and common tendency of any art at the end of a long flowering, and when its forms and concepts have already become accepted as tradition in their grand central themes and essential statements,—so that to wrestle with and define these themes seems no longer the artist's essential imaginative endeavor,—to seek intellectual excitement or edge, and aesthetic freshness, by elaborating the forms in detail and by subtilizing the concepts. And what is true of the art of the two groups, is also true of the themes themselves. The religious themes in the use of which Crashaw follows Marino, Marino himself owes to the same movement in religious literature and meditation which produced the neo-Latin poetry. And to this movement he likewise owes that method of approach to sacred subjects which he and Crashaw have in common.

But in spirit and purpose, and in the temper which animates the detail of their work, Marino and the neo-Latin writers are far apart. To read them side by side is to be struck anew with one of the most fascinating problems in the study of any period of civilization. Across any of the great episodes of civilization falls some one intellectual impulse or dynamic of thought which animates every expression of that civilization—intellectual and imaginative outlook, social consciousness, *mores*, art. And we describe this impulse as the balance of the human spirit achieved by that civilization. But the more intently we gaze at that unity, the more do we perceive in the heart of it the working of those disparate energies which, taking their renewed force from the very dynamic of the balance itself, are preparing to destroy or change it. For within the unity are totally different foci of imaginative or spiritual activity which admit that unity within themselves in very different terms. And in the new energy which may arise out of the pressure of the unity upon one or more of these foci, lie the seeds of growth, of destruction, and of a new balance. So it is with Marino and the epigrammatists, the former creating an energy brief as a flash of summer lightning, while in the latter we see faintly adumbrated something of that sustained intellectual effort and direction which the Jesuits contributed to neoclassicism. For our purpose, we may briefly define the difference as follows: Marino is to the core worldly and sophisticated. Religious practise and the art of religious reflection are to him only part of a gentleman's education and habit. Intellectually, indeed, the Jesuits, too, were of the world; so much so that as Henry James would have said, they were not worldly, they were the world. But Marino's cool intellectuality is trifling and disillusioned, emotionally sophisticated; and his imagery, even in religious poems, is shaped by the aesthetic and intellectual dilletantism and neo-paganism which created his *Adone*, while the imagery and artistic schematism of the epigrammatists, however dry and grotesque, are resonant of the moral purpose which enkindled their intellectual effort (and the scope of which we shall not understand unless we remember that it enabled them to inspire and prepare men like Southwell for the English mission and for martyrdom). Hence with this broad difference of spirit in mind, we ought, if we interpret carefully the evidence of specific imitations and translations, to be able to make the necessary distinctions between the two forces at work in Crashaw's apprenticeship.

There is still a further problem of synthesis to face besides that of the two schools of poetry which Crashaw studied. Poetry is as a whole the most difficult of the arts in which to define influences, and except that of philosophy, the most difficult sphere of intellectual life in which to trace relationships. For poetry is made of the stuff and, unlike the other arts, with the instruments, of all men's consciousness. The painter is, from the moment he takes up the pencil, an artist in some sort aware as an artist of his observation of the technique and method of the pictures he sees; and the influence of this technique and method on him is, therefore, explicit and direct. Not so the poet; to him, from the beginning of articulate thought as a man, the creation and the reception into consciousness of words, rhythms, and images is essential to being; and his imagination is both shaped by these words and rhythms and images, and in its turn is shaping them, so that he is constantly cultivating his own powers of perception and making his own idiom of expression from all that he reads and hears merely as a man, long before he listens with the artist's special ear to a single poem. Crashaw, when he became a student of poetic art, apprenticed himself to the neo-Latin epigrammatists and to Marino; but before his years of apprenticeship, his sensitive being had already grown up in the world of Elizabethan thought and poetry, and above all, one may feel sure, in the enchanting world of Spenser. The spirit of this Elizabethan environment is manifest in Crashaw in many particular passages; manifest also in the sudden spontaneous budding, amid Crashaw's early schematism, of images fresh as young-eyed cherubim; present in sound patterns; felt by the reader, especially in the early poetry, in a pervasive and impalpable Elizabethan ardor; never wholly lost; so luminous that one image will show it,

> Yet when young April's husband showrs
> Shall blesse the fruitfull Maja's bed
> We'l bring the First-born of her flowrs.

Crashaw is, then, an extraordinarily sensitive being, the waters of whose impulse have channelled their way through many and varied rock-beds and bring with them the silt of their far sources, before they form the river of his mature poetry. Yet if we bear these conditions carefully in mind, we can, through a detailed study of the material in hand, realize the broad nature of these influences and watch the fashioning of a poet.

It is with the Latin and Greek epigrams that we are concerned in this chapter. The Greek epigrams, however, are as nearly like the Latin as may be, and do not call for separate consideration. What is said of the Latin epigrams may be held to be said of them likewise. The English epigrams, on the other hand, even though they are translations or versions of the Greek and Latin originals, are quite distinct in manner. They seem to show that Crashaw conceived a totally different style to be suitable to poetry in the vernacular, a style in general much like that of his Marinistic poems and his translations from the Jesuit elegists. Accordingly, though there is no objective evidence for their date, it will be more suitable to consider them with these latter poems.

The Latin epigrams themselves do not, as we have already suggested, form a strictly homogeneous group. For though some certainly of them, and probably most, are school exercises of one particular type, yet a few are based on Marino. The great majority of them, however, are in one style, the broad outlines of which are readily definable. To characterize them in a word, they translate the Bible into Ovid. In this, they form part of that long and strange story of the fascination exerted by Ovid, sometimes moralized, and sometimes in his native guise, over the imaginations of the Middle Ages and the Renaissance, while greater poets sometimes went unstudied,—a story interestingly outlined by Professor H. B. Lathrop in his *English Translations from the Classics.*[2] They embody the spirit and method of Ovid as that was reduced to a system of rhetoric. They are highly rhetorical, first, in their use of dramatic question and answer, whether the figures and objects in the epigram speak to each other, or the author address them in the proud consciousness of his own superior insight; secondly they are rhetorical in their excessive use of violent contrast and of paradox; thirdly in the frequent use of verbal turn or repetition to emphasize the contrast and the paradox, though the paradox itself is not verbal.

> *Spectàsne (ah!) placidìsque oculis mea vulnera tractas?*
> *O dolor! ô nostris vulnera vulneribus!*
> *Pax oris quàm torva tui est! quàm triste serenum!*
> Tranquillus miserum qui videt, ipse facit.[3]

They are melodramatic in their emotions, and they readily attribute emotions and sentiments to inanimate objects. Moreover, of course, all these elements are further stylized when the drama is no longer even suggested by the subject of the particular epigram in hand but is nevertheless gone through as if such dramatization constituted the legal formula for the epigram. Just how Ovid appeared to the writers of such epigrams and just how formalized was the notion of his style is clearly shown in a wellknown handbook. In 1602 Ioannes Buchler à Gladbach prepared, for the second edition of his *Thesaurus Phrasium Poeticarum,* an *Institutio Poetica* ex. R. P. Pontani libris desumpta, in which he derives from that editor of Ovid the following definition of Ovidian style:

> *Virtutes,* & *Artificium Elegorum:* Capvt. xxxvi. Oratio Elegiaca tersa sit oportet, lenis, ingenua, perspicua, morata, tenera, affectibus referta, Pathetica, & sententijs exquisitis minimé obfuscata, atque impedita. Mirificé eam ornant frequentes commiserationes, conquestiones, exclamationes, apostrophae, prosopopeiae, fere fictae personae,

[2] University of Wisconsin Studies in Language and Literature, number 35. (Madison, Wisconsin: 1933).

[3] LUC.10.32. "Sacerdos quidam descendens eadem via, vidit & praeteriit." Richard Crashaw, *The Poems,* ed. L. C. Martin, p. 19.

excursus, & παρεκθάσεις seu breves & cum re aptè cohaerentes digressiones; non modicum eidem decus accedit per allusiones ad Apothegmata. Ornatur etiam inductionibus & exemplis: exemplis, inquam, non modò á simili, verum etiam á dissimili, & contrario interdum ad comparationem adhibebtur. Interijciuntur item sententiae, tum breves, tum acutae, quibus id, quod est propositum, confirmatur. . . .[4]

With a very few exceptions, and these exceptions consisting of elements which could appear only in longer works, the devices listed by Buchler describe the rhetoric of Crashaw's epigrams and of the other neo-Latin epigrammatists. Paradox is the dominant method, giving color to all the other devices. The themes of Crashaw and of the Jesuits deal wholly with religious story, and it is perhaps for this reason, as well as by the mere process of stylization, that they use paradox so frequently; for to them life is a constant paradox between the forms of things and their allegorized meaning, the objects of this world being one extended allegory of the spiritual world; or between the values and ways of life of this world as the man of the world reads and lives it, on the one side, and on the other, the values of the spirit.

*Felix ô! lacrymis (ô Lazare) ditior istis*
*Quàm qui purpureas it gravis inter opes!*
*Illum cùm rutuli nova purpura vestiet ignis,*
*Ille tuas lacrymas quàm volet esse suas!*[5]

The "exempla" the use of which Buchler inculcates, not only from like things but also from unlike, abound. The epigrams also exaggerate the attributions of sentiment to inaminate objects, partly because of the violent nature of the whole rhetoric, partly, we may suppose, as in the case of paradox, because the poet is so vividly conscious of the human meaning within the allegorical significance of objects. The effect of such sentimental attribution is, however, here even more than in Ovid, remote from sensuous suggestion and becomes merely ingenious. It is thoroughly conventional. For instance, Mr. Martin cites in his notes three analogues of Crashaw's famous trope in the epigram on the water

---

[4] I quote from the edition Londini M. DC XXXII, (the eleventh edition, since this is the edition with which it is convenient for me to check), Pp. 453-455.

[5] LUC. 16. "In lacrymas Lazari spretas a Divite" Crashaw, ed. Martin, p. 21.

turned to wine, "*Nympha pudica Deum Vidit*, & erubuit"; the epigrams of Jacobus Biderman yield a fourth analogue; and doubtless there are numerous others. These then are the marks of Ovid as the school-boy's pattern.

Besides this general stylization of the Ovidian rhetoric in the school epigrams which Crashaw studied and wrote, there came to be especially dominant in the Jesuit epigrams and elegies to which Crashaw gave attention at the same time he was also studying Marinism, certain other definitely stylized qualities which likewise owed much to indirect Ovidianism. These additional qualities must be here defined. To begin with, the use of the verbal turn combines with the moral interpretation to make a verbal symbolism not uncommon, as in this from Bernardus Bauhusius Antverpianus,

*Spiritus Sancti* imago, Columba.
Pneuma sacrum niueae quod pinguitur ore columbae
Non est de nihilo, credite; causa subest.
Ille Deus Pacis, volucres hae Pacis; amantque
Candida tecta illae, candida corda Deus.[6]

Side by side with this play on words we find an imagery that likewise has some roots in the habit of constant allegorical interpretation, but that is, as it is worked out in detail, like the verbal turn, also purely ingenious and not interpretative. Thus Bauhusius says of the seven Penitential Psalms that no one can read them without being moved.

Eia, animo procul omne movent ferumque feramque,
Et bibat ex oculis pagina prima tuis.
Deiiciant liquidas tibi vitrea lumina gemmas:[7]

This type of imagery, further, often dwelt with particular emphasis on the physical details of the life of Christ,

*Quisque capillus it exiguo tener alveus amne,*
*Hôc quasi de* rubro *rivulus* oceano.

*O nimiùm* vivae *pretiosis amnibus* undae!
Fons vitae *nunquam verior ille fuit*,[8]

---

[6] *Epigrammatum Libri V*. Editio altera, auctior. (Antverpiae, M.DC. XX) p. 8. That the sacred breath is painted from the mouth of a dove is not without meaning, believe it; there is an underlying cause. He is the God of Peace, these the birds of Peace: white houses they love, the white heart, God.

[7] *Ibid.*, p. 4. Behold from afar with their spirit they move every savage thing, and the first page drinks from your eyes. Their lights (eyes) of glass send down for you liquid gems.

[8] Crashaw. ed. Martin, p. 27. "In Vulnera Dei Pendentis." Each hair goes with a small stream (of Blood) as if a rivulet from this purple ocean. Oh, too living waters of these precious rivers! never more truly was he the fountain of life.
For the more complete expansion of this epigram, see Crashaw's own translation.

Such imagery comes from the extension of the allegorizing tendency when that tendency is mingled with a habit of Ovidian word play; but the word play and the mechanical rhetoric so prevail over the original allegorical intention that the symbolism and the imagery themselves arise out of ingenious wit and do not spring from direct imaginative or emotional experience. They do not, therefore, on the whole, create imaginative experience in the reader, but only excite in him a curious attention.

This mingling of far-fetched ingenuity and of melodramatic rhetoric characterizes, then, the formal style in which Crashaw's epigrams are bound up. And taken singly, his verses, like the others of their kind, are to our modern taste highly rhetorical and chill. The few we have quoted are fair samples of the whole. We cannot, reading them one by one, read ourselves back into the attitude of mind of the world which once found them expressive. When we read them through as a whole, however, we are struck by certain other impressions rising from the cumulative effect of the whole, the cumulative effect having an insistent power to absorb us which no single epigram possesses; and in these impressions we begin to feel the individual spirit of the poet. This spirit is definable in a certain passionate seriousness of intention. The element in Crashaw's epigrams of the moral *sententia,* while not actually large, leaves a weighty and abiding impression, and beneath the gingerbread of the rhetoric, the massed effect of the contrast of two ways of life, two sets of values, strikes deeply on the reader's imagination after the trivial effect of the style has faded.

In this passionate intensity which we cannot illustrate lies the poet who was ultimately to flower in the few great hymns. But the ripening is slow and painful. Crashaw's depth of spirit did not readily free itself or illuminate his rigid techniques. And we must now examine a further influence which tended to bind Crashaw's and other poetry of the day still more tightly in formalism. Not only the mechanical analysis of Ovid, but other aspects of the formal rhetoric of the day as well, could not but affect both the epigrammatists and Marino; and they affected Crashaw both directly to a certain extent and more particularly through these other poets. For this rhetoric constituted an important feature of the school training of the day, and a good bit of Jesuit scholarship was expended upon it. The forms of style created by the rhetoric books deserve, therefore, some attention.

As Donald Leman Clark points out in his *Rhetoric and Poetry in the Renaissance,*[9] Renaissance poetic was deeply tinged with rhetoric and with rhetoric in the single aspect of style. We find in Renaissance rhetoric, accordingly, very elaborate instructions on all details of style, and particularly on such elements as metaphor and simile. Many of the textbooks and handbooks, moreover, instruct in the craft of making metaphors as though this skill were a series of mental gymnastics or evolutions independent both of any substance which the metaphor is to express and of the organic part of the metaphor in any work of art as a whole. It was not so, of course, in the beginning. Aristotle treats both the principles on which the metaphor and simile are formed, (the psychological principles, that is, expressed in formal terms) and the general laws of their aesthetic effects. Moreover, his general principles are closely related to the actual examples of great poetry from which they are drawn, so that in him the harmonious relation of the metaphor to the substance it expresses and to the artistic whole of whose design it is a part is a condition always implied as an important element of his context. Moreover, as a further safeguarding of the organic relation between the metaphor and some larger whole, both in meaning and style, Aristotle says that the art of the metaphor cannot be taught. In its literal meaning, this remark of his states only that the wit to see likeness cannot be taught; but again the whole context of his treatment shows him to mean further that what cannot be taught is the intelligence to find such likenesses as are significant for their acuteness and for the emotional and aesthetic connotations which they carry.

And yet, even with these safeguards of Aristotle's, the detailed analysis of minor elements in the technique of style, even from the point of view of the principles of thought and representation involved, may be a dangerous practice in the hands of the young literary beginner. Anyone who has taught composition to undergraduates is painfully aware how difficult it is to consider with them any aspects of the technique of expression without

[9] New York: 1922.

seeming to turn the whole art of expression into a mere matter of techniques. Separately analyzed and defined, the mere instrumentalities seem to have absolute values as ends, instead of conditional values as means. The dull students will decide with despair that since writing is a matter of mental gymnastics divorced from their experience, they cannot write anything; and the slightly gifted but brash will imagine that since they have double joints and nimble toes, they have, *ipso facto*, a great deal to say. I remember at one time reading a set of blue-books in which a group of freshmen who had been studying description were asked to criticize a number of passages, including one that had been inserted as a horrible example, and that began in some such fashion: His eyebrows were doormats on which all incoming perceptions had to wipe their feet before they gained entrance to the keen gray eyes. Bright pupil after bright pupil characterized the description as excellent; for it had a fundamental image, so and so many metaphors, etc. And it was only, at last, a tough, earthy boy, no writer and no wit, who, after struggling valiantly to define the rhetorical points, broke off with a sudden, "Anyhow, I think this is vulgar."

The danger that the concept of style will become mechanized is even greater when we pass from so fundamental and empirical a study as Aristotle's to a more abstract study; and still greater when we pass on to the handbook.

The Renaissance rhetoricians, except to some extent the very greatest, had not, in their treatment of style, the safeguards of Aristotle, having nothing of his philosophical view. Nor did they in the least remember that the art of using metaphor cannot be taught. On the contrary, they set out to teach it categorically, and seem to have hoped by a minute dialectic of style to create many Thomas Acquinases of poetry.

Among the cardinal virtues of poetry as they taught it was variety. Thus Scaliger says that the function of poetry in *docendo & delectando* can be fulfilled by those who are near to the truth and "*sibiipsis semper conuenientes exequuti fuerint, & operam dederint, vt omnia varietate condiantur.*"[10] And he expresses the

[10] Ivlii Caesaris Scaligeri *Poetices libri septem,* (Lyon): M.D. LXI, Liber III. Capvt xxv, p. 113. "Have always executed their work harmoniously with themselves, have also striven that they might build all with variety."

praise of Vergil that "Igitur quumsemper sit ille sublimi spiritu, & generosa oratione: nusquam tamen est sui similis." This praise is illustrated by a comment on Vergil's diversity and variation in incident and then by a general praise of his variety in figures: "Ac tametsi videtur haec cognitio atque vsus figurarum, tum prudentiam, tum efficaciam, tum suauitatem vel commendare vehementer, vel etiam maxima ex parte conficere atque iccirco post omnes describenda videbatur: ea tamen est eius *cum varietate* necessitudo, vt figurae pené essentia varietas sit."[11]

Scaliger in this is praising Vergil for that rich and varied view of the human scene so important to poetry, and doubtless he has in mind much what Keats intended in his words about *Endymion*, "It will be a test, a trial of my Powers of Imagination, and chiefly of my invention, which is a rare thing indeed—by which I must make 4,000 lines of one bare circumstance and fill them with poetry—" When, however, we come to Vossius' discussion of variety, he seems to feel the whole more mechanically, and his book is much more in the nature of a handbook of instruction than it is of a philosophical discussion. Frequent practice, he says, helps to secure proper expression. One must see how variously everything can be said. This variety, then, will consist not in "verbis simplicibus sed etiam conjunctis,"—that is, in metaphors or periphrases. As an instance of this desirable variety, he lists Vergil's figures for death, of which he gives nine, and goes on to say that Vergil does as well with tempest, grief, rage, war, a ship.[12] This enumeration of instances of variety in figure divorced from any consideration of the context of the figures or of their imaginative beauty, and of diction divorced from meaning, certainly tends to make of variety not a richness of perception and interpretation, but a skilled technical exercise in finding external resemblances. This is reduced to even more of the mechanic exercise in Buchler's digest of Pontanus:

Genera quaedam exercitationis Poeticae, // Capvt x. //
Primum sit illud, unam eandemque rem diversis verbis, eadem, aut

[11] *Ibid.*, Liber III, Capvt xxviii, pp. 119 and 120. "Then, though he is always sublime in spirit and noble in speech, yet he never repeats himself." "And although this knowledge and use of figures seems strenuously to commend both prudence and effectiveness and sweetness or even in large part to create those qualities and therefore it would seem as though it ought to be described last of all yet, such is the need of it with variety that variety is almost the essence of imagery."

[12] Gerardi Joannis Vossii. *De Artis Poeticae Natura ac Constitutione Liber.* Citation from the edition Amstelodami MDCXLVII.

diversa specie carminis eloqui: exempla sit, Amnis glacie concretus, in Appendice Virgiliana diversis modis eleganter descriptus. [A long quotation pp. 419-420] 2. Conducet tractari idem nunc concisè & breviter, nunc amplè & copiosè: nunc propriis, nunc modificatis verbis, nunc simplici, nunc versa, & luminibus insignita oratione. etc[13]

In such an approach to the subject of variety, metaphor becomes, then, an externalized thing. As we have already said, even in a philosophical approach to the subject, it is hard to define the types and modes of metaphor without turning poetic metaphor into any mere process of wit that accurately follows one of certain specific logical formulae of comparison, and without forgetting that the only true test of metaphor lies in its imaginative relation to the object figured and in its aesthetic energy. Thus even Scaliger's definition of figure emphasizes patterns of reasoning or wit rather than power of interpretation and at least suggests that the pivot between the figure and the subject figured lies in their physical outlines, rather than in their organic and functional life or in their emotional context:

> Figura est notionum quae in mente sunt, tolerabilis delineatio, alia ab vsu communi. Notiones voco rerum species externarum, quae per sensus delatae, in animo repraesentantur. Harum specierum lineamenta communia sunt, qualia in rebus ipsis. Igitur oculi cuiuspiam iracundi quum siunt sanguinei, accipiam eos in meam cogitationem, atque à similitudine flammae dicam Inflammatos, & ignem ab ipsis micare. Ecce alia lineamenta, quàm quae vulgò conspicimus. Intelligo autem lineamenta eadem licentia, qua & figurae vox recepta est. nánque in corporibus naturalibus est quantitas, quam gerit substantia. Ea quantitas est finita, is finis eiúsq modus atque praescriptio figura est. Quum igitur dico delineationem, non intelligo lineam nudam, sed eius quoque sobolem circunscriptam superficiem. Praeterea quum colores aliud sunt à superficie: tamen quum superficiem per colores videamus, delineationem hanc & ad eos & ad alia accidenta referemus. Quinetiam quum substantia, qua substantia est, non habeat à superficie circunscriptionem: hoc enim est proprium quantitatis solius: tamen quia aequè atque res omnes aliae praeter Deum, finita est: necessariò admittit aliquam praescriptionem. Cuius

---

[13] *Op. cit.*, p. 419. A certain kind of poetic practice. This is the first, to say the same basic thing in different words, in the same or a different metrical form: an example of this is a stream hardened into ice, which is elegantly described in diverse ways in our Vergilian appendix. In the second place, it is profitable to express the same thing now concisely and briefly, now fully and copiously: now in literal words, now in modified words, now simply (or, directly), now in an expression that is inverted and decorated with lights.

terminus si non est linea, aut à linea: at est aliquid vel illi simile, vel qui similis illa sit; . . .[14]

How this tendency to make of metaphor a matter of physical properties worked itself out in such a handbook as Buchler's we have already seen. What it might still further become is shown in Emanuele Tesauro's *Il Cannochiale*, part of which, showing how the theme of the Magdalen might be elaborated, (the passage is addressed to preachers but will serve for poets) is quoted so effectively by Signor Praz in his *Secentismo e Marinismo in Inghilterra.*[15] The whole treatise so vividly illustrates the geometrical approach to imagery that it is worth quoting a portion of it. Among Tesauro's schematic analyses of metaphors is that of the *simiglianzo analogo di proportione,* of which there are two genera, depending on the *sommo genere analogo.* For example, there is Pericles' figure in which he called the youth of Athens *Primavera della Citta.* This is analyzed as follows:

| | | |
|---|---|---|
| Genere Analogo | Duration Di | Tempo |
| Genere subalterno | Etá humana | Stagion del Anno |
| Specie analoghe | Giouinezza | Primavera |

Tesauro's subdivisions of types of figures and of fields from which metaphors may be drawn run well over one hundred pages. Among them capitolo viii, under the forms of the allegory of proportion, lists the *descrittioni arguti*: If you call the Rose Queen

---

[14] *Op. cit.,* Liber III, Capvt xxx, p. 120. "A figure is an acceptable delineation of the notions which are in the mind, a delineation different from that in common use. By notions I mean the kinds of external objects which are present to the mind, having been brought to it by the senses. There are lineaments common to these different kinds, just as there are in the objects themselves. For instance when the eyes of someone in a rage are blood-shot, I receive them into my consciousness, and from the likeness to a flame, I say that they are inflamed, and that fire gleams in them. There are other lineaments than those we commonly see. For I use the term "lineaments" with the same license as that with which we receive the word "figure." For in natural bodies there is a quantity (or, measure) which the substance supports, this measure is bounded, the figure is the bounds, form, limitation of it. When then I say "delineation (or limitation)," I do not mean the bare outline, but also the superficies of it. More particularly though the colors of an object are a different thing from the superfices of it: yet since we see the superficies through the colors, we refer our delineation to them and to other accidents. Moreover, although substance, *qua* substance, is not circumscribed by a superficies; for this is the property of quantity alone; yet since equally with all other things except God it is finite: it must have some circumscription. And if the boundary of this is not a line, or made by a line, yet it is something else like that or which that is like."

[15] Pp. 220 *et. seq.*

of Flowers, you can list all the circumstances of the rose together with those of the queen as follows:

| Rosa | Raina | |
|---|---|---|
| Pianta eminente | Dignita' sublime. | Substantia. |
| Rossor della foglie | Porpora de Manto | Qualitas |
| Odori | Profumi. | Qualitas |
| Tra' fiori | Tra le Danzelle | Relatio |
| Zefiri aspiranti | Cortidiani ossequosi | |
| Pasce le Api | Premia i buoni | Actio |
| Uccide gli scarabei | Punisce i maluaggi | |
| Sfiorice muor | Muore | |

And so forth at considerable length.[14] Tesauro, with a conscientious glance at his model Aristotle, recognizes (on page 82) that "Egli e' vero nondimeno, che il troppo e troppo. Peroche cosi nella metafore, come nell' altre Voci Pellegrine, hassi a guardar la sante legge del (118) *Decoro*." But this classic admonition is hardly outstanding amid the hundreds of pages of instruction in the ingenious wit of the mechanical metaphor.

The effect of the rhetoric or poetic guide was, then, to emphasize ingenuity in figure, gaudy decoration, and externality. The result was to develop the figure at the expense of the whole. In the large and leisurely movement of the epic poem, with its broad picture of life, the extended simile, which begins with a luminous description of the object figured and then moves on to complete its own beautiful scene before returning to the narrative, is an element of great organic beauty in that it helps to create that ample background scene and that sense of a whole world which are so necessary to the manifold life of the epic. But in the lyric, and particularly in the lyric of personal emotion, where the creation of the emotions depends on intense and instantaneous effect, the poet must concentrate upon the subject and the ideas which are the immediate well-springs of the emotion; and toward them all imagery must speed like an arrow. So in Shakespeare's sensuous lark image

> Yet in these thoughts myself almost despising,
> Haply I think on thee, and then *my state*,

[14] Conte D. Emanuele Tesauro, *Il Cannocchiale Aristitelico, a sia, Idea che serue a tutta l' Arte Oratoria, Lapidaria, et Simbolica, Esaminata co' Principii Del Divino Aristotele. Settima Impressione* Accresciuta dall' Autore . . . (Bologna, MDCLXXV) p. 320. (First published Venezia, 1655).

> Like to the lark at break of day arising
> From sullen earth, *sings hymns at heaven's gate*

the image sinks into the subject and melts away, leaving the reader's spirit standing with the poet at the gate of heaven. And so, too, in Fulke Greville's metaphysical figures, image wings back into subject,

> Life is a top which whipping sorrow driveth.

> For sorrow holds man's life to be her own,
> His thoughts her stage where tragedies she plays
> Her orb she makes his reason overthrown,
> His love foundations of her ruins lays;
> So as while love would torments of her borrow,
> Love shall become the very love of sorrow.

So too in the long image of the forest in storm in A. E. Housman's "On Wenlock edge the wood's in trouble," a poem in which the theme is gradually unveiled through the image until we are conscious only of complete absorption in the storm of man's unquiet life.

But the effect of this rhetoric we have been describing is to concentrate upon the images as ends in themselves, and constantly to forget the theme which they figure, and in so forgetting the theme to shatter the emotion. This rhetorical method was present to some extent in the Latin epigrams of Crashaw, though in them the image still followed fairly closely the configuration of the dialectal moral analysis which was their main substance. The method will be felt with full distinctness in the Jesuit epigrams, even in the few brief examples we have given. It is precisely the method of Marino and of Crashaw's Marinistic poems, and we shall study the operation of it more fully when we consider those poems. For it was through Marino that the style affected Crashaw most obviously. The rhetorics had also, in all probability, a direct influence on Crashaw in other poems than his epigrams, though not in itself a persistent influence. For instance, there is the minor fact that he translated the opening of Heliodorus into pentameter verse. Now Mr. Clark quotes the opinion of Robortelli that poetry might be in either prose or verse, if it were imitation, and instances the point that Robortelli regarded Lucian, Apuleius, and

Heliodorus as poets.[15] Crashaw's fragment of Heliodorus, then, shows his view of verse in this at least, to coincide with that of the rhetoricians. Moreover, the whole system of secondary school training in style rested on the rhetorics.

Another type of handbook which must have exerted an influence in the same direction with that of the rhetorics was the phrasebook of metaphors which grew out of the rhetorical handbook. Vossius, as we have seen, cited a group of passages to illustrate Vergil's variousness in his figures. There were large collections devoted solely to metaphors grouped together under the heads of the objects they figured. To name a few, Susenbrotius' *Epitome troporum ac schematum . . .* was published in England as early as 1562; Fletcher's *Certain very proper and most profitable Similes* in 1595; and the *Bel-vedere or Garden of the Muses* of 1600 contains at the close of each group of sentences a number of similes from English poetry. Such collections as these are in the nature of anthologies or encyclopoedias of quotations rather than handbooks or poet's crutches. The Latin collections of phrases, however, are of this latter sort. Thus Dietrichus Offenbescius points out to young poetic aspirants the usefulness of the *Thesaurus Phrasium Poeticarum* of Joannes Buchler: Those, he says, who do not wish like Icarus to go on uncertain wings or like Phaeton to fall, can shine brilliantly by using this book. And another admirer of the same thesaurus guarantees that it will teach a man to be a poet worthy of the Muses and of Apollo. And, as Mr. Foster Watson points out in his *English Grammar Schools to 1660*, Brinsley in his *Ludus Literarius*, 1612, and Hoole in his *New Discovery of the Old Art of Teaching* both recommend Buchler for use in teaching verse-writing in the schools.[16] Under the article *Lacrymae* in Buchler we find,

> Inania munera mortis. Signa animi moesti. Tepidus ros. Tepidus imber. Lacrymarum rivus. Effusae gravidis uberibusque genis. Uberibus oculis lacrymarum flumina missa. Lacrymae introrsus obortae. Ora rigantes. In ora cadentes. Ora genasque rigantes, humectantes. Rivi more fluentes. Vocis pondera habentes. (Cf. Crashaw's "Sententious showers, ô let them fall,/Their cadence is Rhetoricall.). In ora, more nivis sole madentis sunt.[17]

[15] *Op. cit.*, p. 72.
[16] Page 477 ff.
[17] *Thesaurus Phrasium Poeticarum*, Priore multo accomodatior lucopletior, Opera M, Ioannis Buchleri à Gladbach. (Londoni: M. DC. XXXII). p. 158.

There follows a further long list for *Lacrymare*. Another collection, *Phrases Poeticae sev Silvae Poeticarum Locvtionum Vberrimae*, gives five octavo pages of *Lacrimae* and concludes the list with *Vide Dolor, Luctus, Gemitus*.

Although few of the figures listed in these phrase books have anything of the ingenuity of Crashaw's figures or of the "argutezza" of the neo-Latin epigrams, yet the effect of them when they are gathered together and stripped of their context is, like that of the rhetorics, to emphasize the elements of mere variety and mere physical delineation in metaphor, and to stress the value of mere multiplicity and inventiveness.

These books of phrases are the last element in the first stage of Crashaw's apprenticeship. Phrasebook, rhetorical exercise, Jesuit poetry, all drive in the direction of ingenuity and of somewhat arid wit, and, from a somewhat different starting point, meet with the stylized theatricality of the Ovidian mode. It was a tradition and a technique which, unlike the gracious and humane convention of, let us say, the epitaphs of Ben Jonson or Carew—a convention in which the formal aspect of expression is perfectly bound up in the meaning—laid a heavy burden upon the poet who would wrest it anew to poetry. That earnestness of content and abiding thought and ardor with which Crashaw's epigrams, taken as a whole, impress us find voice in those verses almost in despite of their style. The style is not yet transmuted by them; and Crashaw's further concentration upon styles of the same sort and upon a poet to whom ingenuity was the essence of his spirit, was to render the process of transmutation a long one. And yet the poetry in the epigrams is a significant promise. It is a germ of the spirit alive in the dry earth and under the choking weeds of rhetoric. In the next chapter of Crashaw's history, we shall see how that germ grew even among the still more suffocating weeds of Marinism.

## Chapter IV

## THE TRANSLATIONS

With the study of the translations and of Marinism in Crashaw, we come to Crashaw's English work. We come also from the school-work which was laid upon him, even if gladly accepted, to the work of his choice. In it, the baroque stream is widened by the great influx of Marinism; and at the same time, there rise to meet these foreign sources the clear springs of Spenserianism and of the Elizabethan spirit. Crashaw's most sustained and most important work in this period is the translation of the first canto of Marino's *La Strage De Gl' Innocenti*; and in this and in a few epigrams likewise translated from Marino, the influence of Marino is most specifically felt and can be most clearly traced. These poems, accordingly, we shall study in detail in order to understand the part which Marino played in the development of Crashaw's art. Then secondly, Marinism is apparent in another group of poems expressive of certain religious attitudes and themes which Crashaw to some extent shared with Marino, though none of these poems are translations. Many continental writers besides Marino were busy with the same themes, and a number of these writers were known to Crashaw and aroused his interest. But the presence in this religious work of Crashaw's of a number of specific details drawn from Marino, together with notable analogues in Marino to Crashaw makes clear that among the numerous writers on the Magdalen and on the Crucifixion it was Marino who specially influenced Crashaw. And, in the third place, even where Crashaw did not actually borrow from Marino, the Marinistic type of theme and Marinistic imagery influenced his art. These three aspects of Marino's influence can best be considered separately, although, in fact, the material of the third aspect, the more general influence of Marinism, is very strongly present in the other two.

Crashaw's study of Marino and Italian poetry probably dates, as we have seen, from his undergraduate years, and the *Sospetto d'Herode* (the first canto of *La Strage*) was translated, as Mr. Martin shows, by 1637, and possibly in that year. It was apparently not his first experiment with Marino. For several among the epigrams which seem to derive from Marino were published in 1635, and on internal evidence *The Weeper* and *The Teare* seem to precede the *Sospetto*. The dates are, however, within these general limits, uncertain, and our best method will be to take up first the *Sospetto*, since in that poem the influence is most specific.

In comparing Crashaw's *Sospetto d'Herode* with the first canto of Marino's *La Strage De Gl' Innocenti*, Signor Praz, to whose *Secentismo e Marinismo in Inghilterra* any student of Crashaw and Marinism is, of course, profoundly indebted, points out that Crashaw's poem is far more dramatic, more imaginative and intense, more concrete and rich in imagery than its original. A detailed examination will show the fundamental imaginative processes and aesthetic laws involved in these differences, as well as defining other literary currents which flowed into Crashaw's composition. Crashaw made the translation stanza for stanza with little variation from the original order of the material so that the relationship of the two poems is easy to follow.

Let us define the difference first in the most formal aspects of style. The greater concreteness of Crashaw is present in almost every line. Thus in stanza 4,[1] *pregio* becomes *strong hand, d'inestinguibil foco hà trono* in 6, becomes *a burnisht Throne of quenchlesse fire*; in 7, Satan's eyes are not merely red but *startle the dull Ayre*; in 10, *il tuo splendor primiero* becomes *all the Beauties of thy once bright Eyes*; in 18, the original speaks of *'l duro fren, che l'incatena, e fascia*; this becomes *what fatall strings, Eternally bind each rebellious limbe*; in 50, *facelle empie, e funeste* smoke as *sulphur-breathed Torches*; 51 is very much more specific in its account of the heritage of the throne, 66 is much more descriptively dramatic both in its detail and in its rhetoric. The result of this concreteness is not merely more sensuous richness, but more intensity of tone as well, an intensity which Crashaw further enhances by his frequent use of adjectives of sentiment. Thus in stanza 26, in the line

And the gay starrs lead on their Golden dance

---

[1] Passages from Crashaw are cited from Mr. Martin's edition of the *Poems*, (Oxford. 1927); the edition of Marino is *La Stage De Gl' Innocenti* Del Cav. Marino (In Venetia. M. DC. LXIV.).

(che non poss' io torre à Natura il seggio
E mutare à *le Stelle ordine, e corso,*
Perche' tanti del Ciel sinistri auspici
Diuenisser per me *lieti, e felici?)*[2]

it is the combined adjectives of color and of tone, acting upon each other, which call the scene to life. And stanza 45 is another example of the focus achieved through the use of more specific words than Crashaw found in his original to emphasize the sentiment or tone of the picture described.

Crashaw is not merely more concrete and more atmospheric in his use of specific detail, but he loves also to embroider elaborately scenes and emotions not present in Marino. Among examples of simple pictorial elaboration are the *golden-winged Herald* (*Nuntio celeste*) of stanza 13; the *momentary wing Of lightning* (*balena*) in 47; the elaborate picturization of Vengeance in 40-43, beginning,

There has the purple *Vengeance* a proud seat,
Whose ever-brandisht Sword is sheath'd in blood.
About her *Hate, Wrath, Warre,* and *slaughter* sweat;
Bathing their hot limbs in life's pretious flood.
There rude impetuous Rage do's storme and fret:
And there as Master of this murd'ring brood,
Swinging a huge Sith stands impartiall Death,
With endlesse businesse almost out of Breath.

V'hà la vendetta in sù la soglia, e'n mano
Spada brandisce insanguinata ignuda,
Havi lo sdegno, e co'l Furor insano
E la Guerra, e la strage anhela, e suda.
Con le minaccie sue fremer lontano
S'ode la Rabbia impetuosa, e cruda,
E nel mezzo si vede in vista acerba
La gran falce rotar morte superba.[3]

There are, too, the wonderful wings of Satan in stanza 18; greatest of all the call to Lucifer in 30:

Art thou not *Lucifer?* hee to whom the droves
Of Stars, that guild the Morne in charge were given?

[2] Why can I not seize from Nature her throne and change the order of the stars and their course, whereby so many evil auspices of heaven would become through me glad and fortunate?

[3] There was vengeance on the threshold and in her hand she brandished a bloody unsheathed sword. There was wrath, and mad Fury, with her, and War, and massacre pants and sweats. Madness impetuous and cruel is heard, fuming her threats far off, and in the midst in bitter view proud death is seen, swinging his great scythe.

The nimblest of the lightning-winged Loves?
The fairest, and the first-borne smile of Heav'n?
Looke, in what Pompe the Mistresse Planet moves
Rev'rently circled by the lesser seaven,
Such, and so rich, the flames that from thine eyes,
Oprest the common-people of the skyes.

Ah non fe'tu la creatura bella,
Principe già de' fulguranti Amori,
Del Matutino Ciel la prima stella,
La prima luce de gli alati Chori?
Che come suol la Candida facella
Scintillar frà le lampadi minori,
Così ricco di lumi alti celesti
Frà la plebe de gli Angeli splendesti.[4]

This picturization often takes the form of personification or miniature allegory, as in the opening lines of stanza 3, in 4, *Thy Fames full noise, makes proud the patient Earth* (*onde memoria al mondo resti*), or in 5, *The Worlds profound Heart pants* (*in mezzo al cor del mondo*), and in the famous flower stanza, 48,

The field's faire Eyes saw her, and saw no more,
But shut their flowry lids for ever.

(Parvero i fiori intorno, e la verdura
Sentir forza di peste.)[5]

The floriate style is in these passages purely decorative; it is not central, that is to say, to the telling of the story or to the assertion of the theme. For the sake of the decoration Crashaw is willing to delay the action by dissipating our attention upon delights that are irrelevant to the effect of the whole,—irrelevant except in so far as all aesthetic experience in a poem is part of the total sentiment. Even where the detail is centrifugal, however, it has this living relation to the poem, that it calls the whole into realized sensuous being. In this sensuous reality it is very different from the elaboration of Marino, even where he is elaborate. But Marino's characteristic elaboration is not to be found indeed in *La Strage*; (perhaps in a long religious poem like *La*

[4] Ah, art thou not that fair creature, once chief of the lightening Loves, the first Star of the Morning Heaven, the first light of the winged choirs? who as the White planet gleams among the lesser lamps thus rich with high divine lights did gleam forth among the common people of the Angels?

[5] The flowers and the verdure all about seemed to feel the might of a pestilence.

*Strage* he looked to the severity of Dante's style as in some sort his classical standard and subdued his own style to the simplicity of that standard). And it is worth while, therefore, to turn aside for a moment to see it in some other narrative poem:

> Con flagello di rose insiemo attorte,
> Ch' avea groppi di spine, ella il percosse,
> E de' bei membri, onde si dolse forte,
> Fe' le vivaci porpore più rosse.
> Tremaro i poli, e la stellata Corte
> A quel fiero vagir tutte si mosse.
> Mossessi il Ciel, che più d'Amor infante
> Teme il furor che de Tifeo Gigante. . . .
>
> Pianse al pianger d'Amor la mattutina
> Del Re de' lumi ambasciatrice stella,
> E di pioggia argentata e cristallina
> Rigò la faccia rugiadosa e bella
> Onde da viva perle accolte in brina
> Potè l'urna colmar l' Alba novella.
> L'Alba che l' asciugò col vel vermiglio
> L'umido raggio al lagrimoso ciglio. . . .
>
> In bionde anella di fin' or lucente
> Tutto si torce e si rincrespa il crine;
> De l'ampia front in maestà ridente
> Sotto gli sorge il candido confine.
> Un dolce minio, un dolce foco ardente
> Sparso tra vivo late e vive brine
> Gli tinge il viso in quel rossor che suole
> Prender la rosa infra l'Aurora e 'l Sole.[6]

Marino elaborates with the energy of intellectual ingenuity rather than of sensuous preoccupation. Whatever the delights of such passages (and to Marino's world they were great), we do not by virtue of the detail live the scenes more fully; whereas the great-

---

[6] Adone, Canto I. stz. 17, 22, 42, (Firenze, n.d., Adriano Salani). With a whip of roses twisted together, that had bunches of thorns, she struck him, and whereat he wailed loudly, she made the living purple of his limbs more red. The poles trembled and the starry courts at that proud cry all stirred. Heaven moved, that fears more the rage of infant Love than that of the Giant Typhus. . . .

At the cry of Love cried the morning star, the ambassadress of the King of Lights, and with a silver and crystal shower she traced that dewy and fair face wherewith the new Dawn might fill her urn with living pearls gathered in hoar-frost. The Dawn who with a crimson veil wiped from her tearful brow the moist beam. . . .

In blond ringlets of fine gold all his hair twisted and curled. Below them rose the white boundary of his ample forehead in smiling majesty. A sweet paint, a sweet burning flame scattered between living milk and living rime, tinged his face in that blush which the rose is wont to take between the Dawn and the sun.

est of Crashaw's elaborations awaken and fill the senses with a living world.

Such elaborations in Crashaw and their divergences from Marino color the whole tone of his poem. They are not casual, but form part of a distinct and consciously chosen style, the main elements of which may be readily defined, the style as a whole manifesting the inflow of Spenserianism. These elements include sensuousness always lighted by sentiment and human meaning, animism, and personification;—elements illustrated, for example, in the house *her's'd about* with a wood, in the orchestration of wind and water,

> The winds sighes timed-bee
> By a black Fount, which weeps into a flood.

the plaintive epithet sustaining the sentiment in "Pale proofe of her fell presence." In adjectives of sentiment the poem is very rich, as, to name only a few more, *"Th' obseqious handmaids* of thy *high command," "The frighted stars* tooke *faint experience,"* "There has the *purple Vengeance* a *proud* seat," "care's *unquiet* sting." And sentiment plays at all times an important part in Crashaw's development of his sources. Indeed, the floriate passages as a whole seek to suggest the theme to us in a sentiment rising like vapor from the abundant sense impressions. In so doing, they do not rely on one sense alone. Sound sensations as well as sight abound, offering themselves to us both in images of sound and in the elaborate music of the verse itself. One or two examples of this verse music will show how carefully the aesthetic effects are planned, and how softly they fuse with the other elements to form one temper. As we have just noted, adjectives of sentiment are essential to the temper of this style; and it is very frequently around these adjectives that Crashaw builds his music, playing on them in alliteration, or assonance, or vowel slide, as in the last line of the fiftieth stanza,

> And with soft feet searches the silent roomes.

Even more rich is the last line of 21, with its reversal of "l" and "f" and "e" and "i" sounds in *life, it, fraile, livery*; a harmonic effect intensified and enhanced by the contrast with these sounds of "e" and "s" sounds in other members of the antithetic phrases:

And life it selfe wea're Deaths fraile Livery.

This floriate style is very different from anything in Marino; and it is rooted in something more fundamental than a difference of technique. It is, indeed, a deliberate technical style; but no technique, though it copy the manner, can achieve the effect. When we have done analyzing the component formal elements in such passages, we are aware that in Crashaw they draw their energy not from any method of expression but from an intensity of the sentiment, which made him turn spontaneously to Spenser and that in many passages it is this sentiment that he elaborates rather than the mere picture, as in stanza 8. In stanza 30 already cited (Art thou not *Lucifer*) sentiment and picture are inseparable as the convex and concave of a circumference. A comparison of the eighteenth stanza with its original might almost serve as a definition of the difference between the mechanics of poetic imagery and poetry itself.

Ai nuoui mostri, à i non pensati mali
L'aversario del ben gli occhi converte,
Nè men, ch'à Morte, à se stesso mortali
Già le piaghe antevede espresse e certe,
Scotesi, e per volar dibatte l'ali,
Che'n guisa hà pur di due gran vele aperte,
Ma'l duro fren, che l'incatena, e fascia,
Da l'eterna prigion partir no 'l lascia.[7]

Strucke with these great concurrences of things,
Symptomes so deadly, unto Death and him;
Faine would hee have forgot what fatall strings,
Eternally bind each rebellious limbe.
Hee shook himselfe, and spread his spatious wings:
Which *like two Bossom'd sailes embrace the dimme*
*Aire*, with a dismall shade, but all in vaine,
Of sturdy Adamant is his strong chaine.

This passage in Marino is too indifferent in its moral and intellectual temper to approach the grand severity of similar descriptions in Dante. And it fills out the spiritual vacancy with mechanical detail. Marino belonged to an over-educated, a jaded world which

[7] At these new prodigies, at these unthought of ills, the adversary of good turned aside his eyes, already he foresaw the wounds express and certain, no less mortal to him than to Death, he drew back and in order to fly beat his wings, which he has in the form of two great open sails, but the hard bridle which chains and binds him up, did not let him depart from his eternal prison.

used its sensations, if it used them at all, either for the play of wit, or as here, for an arid verbal evolution. Crashaw, on the other hand, though not matured to anything of Dante's spiritual grandeur, is never dry or hollowly witty; he is first of all a person filled with young Elizabethan ardor, a person of intense and fluid feeling. And for that ardor, Spenser is his great exemplar.

In these passages we have just read, and which are so Spenserian, Crashaw's style springs so spontaneously from his feeling that even though they sacrifice the whole to the detail, still the lines "surprise us not with themselves but with their subject." This is by no means always true. Consider, for instance, the forty-eighth stanza,

> Heav'n saw her rise, and saw Hell in the sight.
> The field's faire Eyes saw her, and saw no more,
> But shut their flowry lids for ever. Night,
> And Winter strow her way; yea, such a sore
> Is shee to Nature, that a generall fright,
> An universall palsie spreading o're
>     The face of things, from her dire eyes had run,
>     Had not her thick Snakes hid them from the Sun.

Compared with its original, the lines are richly concrete, but the figure,—a forced personification to begin with—is ingeniously developed beyond the genuine perception from which it springs; and in this centripetal ingenuity, if it is unlike Marino in its concreteness, the style is preeminently Marinistic, both in taste and in technique.

That Crashaw did not rest in mere ingenuity in his images, as Marino chiefly did, but converted ingenuity to more imaginative uses, a study of his metaphors will show. But the ingenuity of them is what first overwhelms us. Metaphor and semi-personification are so common in Crashaw's poem that to illustrate, one is tempted to quote the poem entire. One might almost say that nothing but the verb *to be* appears as its simple self. From such living pictures and spontaneous personifications as spring naturally from the sensuous consciousness of life, and the personal perspective of the imagination, pictures such as most of those we have just been reading, or as this of "(Night hangs yet heavy on the lids of Day)," or "Swift as the momentary wings" of lightning, we pass rapidly into ingenious figures of intellect. The fire is blown up not by *bellows*, but by *artificiall lungs*; Vengeance comes to Satan:

> She comes to th' King and with her cold hand slakes
> His Spirits, the Sparkes of Life, and chills his heart,
> Lifes forge.
>
> (Al Re dal sonno opresso, e soprafatto
> S'accosta, e 'l cor con fredda man gli stringe.)[8]

The coming of Spring as a symbolizing of the Nativity is apocalyptic enough in Marino, but in Crashaw the literal sense in which he plays upon the delights of the manna, milk, and so forth suddenly lands the dizzy reader in Auerbach's cellar, *new-broaching the Mountaines*! These figures afford neither sensuous interpretation of the object they figure, nor emotional expression of it; nor, on the other side, does the scientific fact related in the figure serve to analyze some psychological condition, or some human relationship, as do Donne's figures with the result that in Donne the grotesque context of the figure is lost in the complex context of the thought. The grotesqueness of the connotations in Crashaw is increased, too, by the witty spinning out of the figure,—a spinning out which often depends on verbal suggestion. If in Marino the walls of Vengeance are hung with tools of wrath, in Crashaw they are *anvills of torments*; and if in Marino the attendants have curls of winding snakes for hair, in Crashaw, their *lockes are beds of uncomb'd snakes*. If in Marino, in an almost unconscious figure of common speech one *traces* the counsels, in Crashaw, he traces them *by the low Footsteps of their Effects*.[9] Far more rich and living than Marino, Crashaw by this purchasing agent's prodigality sometimes makes his theme smaller and more limited than that of Marino. As our attention follows the evolution of the wit, even the sensuous experience evades us. And it is perhaps because of this sensuous aridity that Crashaw can mix figures so casually and absurdly,

---

[8] She greets the king overwhelmed and oppressed with sleep, and presses his heart with her cold hands.

[9] Reading them, one is reminded of the tale of the intellectual fool who being sent out to purchase a fowl and returning empty-handed, thus justified himself; He went first to the butcher-shop. "Have you a nice chicken?" "Nice chicken? Yes, see here how fat it is." But then if fat is the desirable quality, why bother with the chicken. He went to the grocer's. "Have you any good fat?" "Good fat? See here, it's just like honey." But why then fat? He went to the bee-keepers. "Have you any nice honey?" "Nice honey? Isn't this just as smooth as oil?" But then, why bother with honey. He went on. "Have you any nice oil?" "Nice oil? See here. This is as clear as water." But then if water is the desired thing, why bother to buy oil? And there is water at home.

> What busy motions, what wild Engines stand
> On tiptoe in their giddy Braynes?

and shift them so rapidly and confusedly,

> Mappe of Heroick worth! whom farre and wide
> To the beleeving world Fame boldly sings:
> Deigne thou to weare this humble Wreath that bowes,
> To be the sacred Honour of thy browes.

> In this sad House of slow Destruction,
> (His shop of flames) hee fryes himselfe, beneath
> A masse of woes.

These images, so concrete in their separate detail, are in their whole context the reverse of concrete. Neither senses nor imagination can make anything visible or palpable of them. They shatter that synthesis of intellectual and sensuous perception which it is the function of supreme metaphor to achieve. In the lines

> Love's not time's fool, though rosy lip and cheeks
> Within his bending sickle's compass come,

the figure cannot be literally perceived, but it is directly and intensely luminous to the imagination, each element being touched just so lightly as to be both fully realized, and yet subdued to the whole which it interprets. But in Crashaw the figures exist for their own ingenuity. Thus in him side by side with rich sensuousness and ardor of feeling and a manner consonant with these, is a literary technique consisting of extreme wit, and of figures built mathematically by ingenuity without feeling or power of naturalistic interpretation. This type of wit is characteristic of Marino's *La Strage*, but it is multiplied a thousandfold by Crashaw until it produces verse wholly different from Marino's. Crashaw's exuberant confusion of images is remote from Marino's sophisticate clarity of intellect. And yet the insensate ingenuity represents the technique coming to Crashaw directly from Marino, and to both from the rhetoric and the handbook.

If the arid wit were all, to understand its nature would not be important. In spite of it, Crashaw's poem somehow lives and has a kind of life in its very imagery. The concrete images, as we have said, are spread so unrestrainedly, mixedly, and without regard to their congruity in thought or feeling with what they figure, that they lose all sensuous reality. They leave us satiate and hardened. But strangely, these images, so hardened into mere words, begin, as we grow accustomed to them, to take on a new life of their own as abstractions. The poet seems searching for a new *abstract* vocabulary of thought that shall have a more living meaning than the old general language of ideas. Some of the metaphors within metaphors will show this. Stanza 2 shifts through a bewilderingly rapid series of metaphors to the lines,

> Deigne thou to weare this humble Wreath that bowes,
> To be the sacred Honour of thy Browes.

The basic figure in these lines is that of the poem as a wreath of honor. This is already a complex image, for the wreath itself is in its origin already a symbol, that of honor. Yet the figure is immediately clear and is not uncommon. So far Marino. But in Crashaw "wreath" is further personified, as if it were not a figure, but had become the name of a quality, the quality of honor. "Wreath" is no longer, then, a concrete term in Crashaw, it is hardly even a symbol, but has become an abstract term, a new synonym for "honor." This abstract term is now re-personified, and in this personification "bowes, to be the sacred Honour of thy brows." Again in stanza 25 there is a slight but significant change from the original. Marino says,

> E d'eterna mestitia espresso aviso:
> Come suol di letitia aperto segno
> Essere in Cielo il lampo, in Terra il riso,[10]

In Crashaw this becomes,

> The forehead's shade in Griefs expression there,
> Is what in signe of joy among the blest
> The faces lightning, or a smile is here.

where *lightning* is not a sensible image as in Marino but has become a symbol and almost an abstract term for the pure idea of that radiance of which originally it is merely a type of supreme example. So, too, in 29 Marino says unadornedly,

> Che poscia vincitor sotterra scende
> Ricco de ricche, e gloriose palme

[10] Is the express token of eternal sorrow: as lightning is wont to be the open sign of joy in Heaven, and laughter on Earth.

> Che vibrando quà giù le fulgid' armi
> Ne le miserie ancor venga à turbarmi?[11]

In Crashaw, the *arms rebuke* his eyes (two different concrete figures mixed) and *dazzle* his *dark Mysteries* (a mixture of concrete verb and abstract noun). Here *arms* signifies the concept of vengeance, *eyes* the perceiving mind, *dazzle* and *dark* the contrasting concepts of good and evil.

Thus Crashaw does not rest in the ingenuity of Marino. He is, however indirectly, dealing with ideas and things where Marino only deals with forms. The mode of expression which he creates is, in a sense, still more complex in its evolution than that of Marino, and still more ingenious in its outer form; but within the maze of the ingenuity he is striving for a new contact with meaning. If we glance for a moment at the morphology of a traditional symbol, the operation of Crashaw's imagination will be more clear. The lily, because of what it means to the senses and imagination as a simple experience, was used in the early Middle Ages as a simile for the Virgin; thence by frequent use it became a symbol, taking on in that form not merely the significance of its own sensuous beauty but something of the abstract idea of purity. This addition of meaning is the essential difference between the simile or metaphor and the symbol. What we feel about the flight of the lark at sunrise in Shakespeare's twenty-ninth sonnet depends directly on the flight of the lark; and our realization of the poet's state is an immediate transfer in our imagination from our emotion about the lark's flight. But what we now feel about the Easter lily is not directly a sensuous response to the *lily*, but rather a complex of what we feel about the flower and what we feel about the Virgin and purity; for the lily has become a name and a sign for the mingled concepts of the Virgin and of purity. Such a name is a valuable addition to poetic language, or the language of thought proceeding through emotion, because as a single word for a highly complex concept it enables us to verbalize in one flash what is one in consciousness; and because, since it is still a sense word, the original sense impression still clings to it together with the memory of its growth through image to symbol, and these sense impressions and mem-

[11] Why then does the victor descend below the earth, with rich and glorious palms, why striking his gleaming arms here below does he come to trouble me further in my misery?

ories add intensity to the meaning. The symbol is thus in a sense *the name of a concept,* and a highly complex concept, which is somehow yet not *abstract.* Such words are of incalculable importance to poetry, especially to the poetry of sophisticated worlds.

Ideas and relationships are among the most powerful and significant values to man and therefore among the most powerful and significant springs of emotion; and hence if they can be vividly and concentratedly realized, they are among the most powerful instruments of lyric creation. For instance, Donne seeks to get at emotion directly through ideas, though, like a lawyer pleading from analogy, he defines his idea through a physical object or fact often not in itself containing any emotional energy, as in the "compass" image. Crashaw, on the other hand, being of an ecstatic habit, chooses, like the makers of the lily symbol, to embody his idea in an object of sharp sensuous color and emotive power. This emotive power, or complex of suggestions, he uses as a sign, or metaphor, of his concept. Thereby he makes that single object the abstract *name* for the spiritual or intellectual concept he would express. But, it cannot be too often stressed, this sense image which he uses in his metaphor is to represent an idea, and not primarily a sense impression; it is the symbol of an idea. And the basic emotion which Crashaw seeks to create in us is to spring not from the image, but directly from the idea.

There is, however, this important difference between the symbol of the lily and those of Crashaw. The lily is an image which has become a symbol and a concept first through universal delight in the flower,—a profoundly direct and simple experience too—and then through a corporate and traditional body of thought and through widespread usage. Its meaning is as traditional, though not so dry and abstracted, as the meaning of the word *sincere,* of whose metaphorical origin as the hall-mark on pure marble we are no longer aware. The full significance of the traditional meaning and common experience with relation to immediacy of communication in a symbol-image can be realized if we compare the experience of a person of literary training and that of a person of literary naïveté with regard to the same image. I have seen a class of college sophomores to whom the opening stanza of Arnold's *Requiescat,*

> Strew on her roses, roses,
> And never a spray of yew.
> In quiet she reposes;
> Ah would that I did too.

communicated nothing of either feeling or idea, because *rose* carried only its literal meaning—and in this region roses are not common garden flowers, nor are hothouse roses a frequent experience to these students—and *yew* carried no meaning whatever, unless that it was a member of the vegetable kingdom. To a more mature group of undergraduates, Shirley's

> The drum is silent, but the lute
> Shall whisper what you will.

conveyed an idea, but no sensuous experience, and evoked no atmosphere and no flood of feeling.

Now Crashaw's symbols, in such metaphors as we have been considering, belong not merely for the inexperienced but for all readers to a group of symbols not created for them by tradition and by common experience of the outer world. Other images in poetry there are not enriched by long use, but so strongly suggested by universal human experience that they will spring up in literatures wide apart in time and place. For instance there is hardly likely to be any literary connection between Homer's epithet for the sea, ἀτρύγετος, *the unvintaged,* and the lines of *Ol' man River* that "He don't plant taters, he don't plant cotton; he just keeps rollin' along." Such figures carry along with them their own sense of belonging to the whole of human society. But Crashaw's symbols spring chiefly out of his own personal experience and associations, sometimes, though not always, from the most individual elements in his personality. By no means always. For we must remember constantly that he is part of a widespread movement to order the objects of this world as a diagrammatic and dialectic scheme of another. This other is in the sophisticate, a world of wit; more universally, in the religious, the world of the spirit. And many of his symbols are the product of his participation as an individual in that religious movement. Some of the images which, when we are reading Crashaw, strike us as most characteristically and peculiarly Crashaw's, surprise us by turning up in another poet. Compare, for instance, Crashaw's "Ears (those tumultuous shops of noise)" with Drummond of Hawthornden's description of the world as "This loathsome Shop of Sinne"; and his "Cleare unwrinckled song" of the nightingale, or his "cleare and all unwrinckled face" with Henry More's "Heaven Smiles without wrinckle" (from *The Triumph*); or his frequent figures of incense to suggest ecstasy or immanence with More's "All the substance of our Souls Up in clouds of Incense rolls" (from *The Philosopher's Devotion*). Even a turn so characteristic of Crashaw—but one cannot be sure how far the intense individuality lies in the wonderful spring of the music—a turn so characteristic as

> Eyes are vocall, Tears have Tongues,
> And there be words not made with lungs;
> Sententious showers, ô let them fall,
> Their cadence is Rhetoricall.

finds an echo in Milton's

> For sure so well instructed are my tears,
> That they would fitly fall in order'd characters.

But the drive of sensuous energy which creates these symbols out of the mere diagrams of wit which in their original rhetoric and in Marino they were, and turns them into true complexes of interwoven sensation and emotion, true concepts of imagination rather than of wit,—this drive Crashaw develops out of his very special experience. This originality costs him dear; for, coming thus from the most special element in the poet's personality, they have not for others the expressiveness of the symbols which spring from the common sensations and emotions.

This highly personal symbolism raises, too, very fundamental questions of the nature of poetry as a function of the mind. Poetry is, indeed, thought or organization of experience proceeding through emotion, and Crashaw was concerned to realize the ultimate thought carried by his symbols, and not their value as picture or sensation. But what exactly we mean by thought proceeding through emotion will depend upon our view of human nature. When intellection—the explicit formulation, that is, of observations and concepts, and then the proceeding from these formulations to new concepts based upon them—when intellection becomes too abstract, there are two dangers; first, the danger either that the observation and the concepts with which we begin may be false or incomplete abstractions from reality or that the process of reaching new conclusions from them,—being unchecked by renewed comparison with experience—may be merely verbal, or at least imperfectly logical. And, second, if we think of the communication of our thoughts, there is the danger that these concepts and conclusions may indeed enter another mind to which they are being communicated but, however deftly they may be manipulated by that mind, may merely rest as formulations upon the surface of it without being digested into the personality or absorbed into true thought. These dangers, as will be seen from what we have already said of symbols and of their endeavor to articulate general concepts which still remain concrete, it is the function of poetry both as thought and as communication to avoid. It seeks to "think" by a movement of actual experience,—experience both sensuous and reflective—creating life-giving air from oxygen and hydrogen. Perhaps one may express it by saying that poetry organizes the varying elements of concrete experience into ever larger and more comprehensive wholes; and that at the points where groups of elements or of experiences come together into such organic wholes, which have a meaning, or an insight, larger than the sum of their parts, sensation and emotion pass into thought. Poetry thus creates and communicates organized states of consciousness.

But men and societies can do strange things with the consciousness. Its functioning and the activity or quiescence of its full energies and potentialities seem to be conditionable. If we conceive of each individual personality as realizing itself most fully in emotions and complexes of emotion that are ends in themselves, without universal quality or external reference, poetry will express one sort of consciousness. If, however, we conceive of the individual state of consciousness as participating, through its organized experiences, in something universal for human nature, and having reference to absolutes, what poetry seeks to express will be different. But in this latter case, again, there may be several still different concepts of the personality. We have said that poetry organizes the varying elements of personal experience into ever larger and more comprehensive wholes, and that at the point where groups of experiences come together into such organic wholes, sensation and emotion pass into thought. Is this organization at its most significant at the point where it is a complex of particular sensations and emotions such as Shelley seeks to realize in the *Hymn to Intellectual Beauty?* Or is there a still larger synthesis which organizes these complexes of sensation and emotion into yet more comprehensive wholes; wholes which include generalizations (these generalizations are, of course, concrete generalizations, still including the sensations and emotions out of which they are made, as the living fruit and flower include the elements they draw from earth and air and sun) and reflections, as in Shakespeare's sonnets or plays? Take as an instance of this synthesis the seventy-third sonnet, "That time of year thou mayst in me behold," with the gradual emergence of the concept of death through the three figures, a concept that grows more explicit and more luminous in each of the figures, the personal sensations and emotions of the moment and those of the past blending together and enlarging into universal reflection, until the concept of death and the personal passion which applies this thought of death to a friend unite to articulate the idea of the couplet. And this living thought of the couplet, thus emerging out of concrete experience, evokes the final far-echoing emotion.

Symbolism may be the instrument for realizing any of these views of the human personality. It may realize some one consciousness as a solipsism; it may express complexes of emotion felt to be common and significant to all men; or it may symbolize concepts which relate all men to each other and to the universe. Symbolism as an instrument of thought or expression peculiarly seeks, as we have seen, to express concepts or states of consciousness that are yet not abstractions. The universal symbol, such as that of the *lily*, invariably is the product of the third of these mental states. The individual symbol may be this universal symbol in process of creation, or on the contrary it may be so tied up in the course of its generation with the minutae of the personal accidents of living that it must remain purely personal as communication, giving the reader but such a fragment of the poet's experience as his special intimacy with the poet allows. Hence the concepts which such personal symbols embody may seek to communicate any of the three views of personality we have defined. In Crashaw there are elements which communicate only personal and fleeting complexes of emotion; as he develops, however, he essays more and more to communicate universal aspects of emotion, drawing their energy and their scope from a great tradition, but expressing in large measure merely what is personal in his participation in this tradition.

Whether he expresses the unique moment of emotion or the larger whole into which emotion may open, an additional difficulty in Crashaw's poetry lies in the fact that he has not yet learned to give us the essence of his experience and prune away the adventitious or the momentary in it. In general, in Crashaw's early poems especially, we are retarded by the difficulty that in this type of poetic expression Crashaw is just beginning to find himself. His symbolism is mingled both with sensuous images and with that trivial exuberance of ingenious wit which is at the moment the deliberate habit of his style. So thickly and confusedly are the impressions strewn that the result is merely kaleidoscopic.

Yet the difficulties lie in the technique and not in the spirit of what Crashaw sought. Under the play of the rhetoric he is reaching for an intensely-felt reality. We have all felt with impatience at times how arid is our language of ideas, if we would think of anything warmer than mathematics; how powerless is our abstract vocabulary to carry with it any living sense of the particular experiences from which the general concept springs, and in which lie the validity and living meaning of the general concept. And in our discontent we are teased with the awareness how it might be otherwise. Sometimes when we are translating from a foreign language, parallel formations in the two languages will wake us suddenly to a sense of the concrete reality in the worn abstraction. The poet peculiarly of all men who use speech feels the need of a language for wholes, for universalities, which remains concrete. To Crashaw, whose approach to the world of thought was through rapture, this need was very special.[12] Perhaps in that need lay, largely, for him, the attraction of a new style. At the same time, in that need lay the imaginative energy which sought to transform the barren ingenuity of his chosen model Marino.

---

[12] A very interesting discussion not of Crashaw, but of the problem of speech, will be found in Owen Barfield's *Poetic Diction, a study in meaning* (London: 1928).

Stanza 6 of the *Sospetto* shows mingled the naturalistic vividness, the ingenious wit, and the feeling which transmuted the wit to symbolism.

> The Iudge of Torments, and the King of Teares:
> Hee fills a burnisht Throne of quenchlesse fire:
> And for his old faire Roabes of Light, hee weares
> A gloomy Mantle of darke flames, the Tire
> That crownes his hated head on high appeares;
> Where seav'n tall Hornes (his Empires pride) aspire.
> And to make up Hells majesty, each Horne
> Seav'n crested *Hydra's* horribly adorne.

This tendency to symbolism transforms to some degree all the imagery of an ingenious type in the *Sospètto.* The transformation is carried further by the number of special and oft repeated symbols and figures which Crashaw introduces into his translation. In stanza 30 of Marino the *loves* are transferred from worldly to heavenly mythology.[12a] Crashaw takes over this mythology, but he does not leave it as he found it. In 16, where Marino speaks in direct and worldly terms,

> Vede. . . .
> scoppiar quanti
> V'ha d'illecito amor nefandi amanti.[12b]

Crashaw generalizes him term *loves* so that the word at least suggests, if it does not explicitly designate, not mere moments of passion, but ardor as a principle (here turned to evil):

> Hee saw the Nest
> Of pois'nous and unnaturall loves, Earth-nurst;
> Toucht with the worlds true *Antidote* to burst.

And in the last line of 3 *Loves*, which does not appear at all in the original, it is definitely used in that symbolic meaning.

> Immortall Hony for the Hive of Loves.

Summer and winter have been for mankind perennial symbols of joy and sorrow, well-being and ill fate. In stanzas 14 and 48 of

---

[12a] Signor Praz' discussion of the transfer of figures from pagan mythology to Christian story in Italian verse (*op. cit.*, chapter xvii) is most interesting. Crashaw makes a quaint transfer. In the Latin poem in defense of *Spes* and *Dilectio,* he pictures *Amor*, the love of God, with bow and quiver.

[12b] He saw . . .discover how many wicked lovers illicit love has there.

Crashaw's poem,—in neither case are they present in his original—they are personified symbols of *spiritual* blessing or loss. Satan reflects on the events connected with the birth of Christ which he has seen.

> Hee saw a vernall smile, sweetly disfigure
> Winters sad face.

By ingenious extension of this symbol, *flowers* likewise becomes a symbol name for spiritual radiance, as in the first line of the seventeenth stanza, and in the connotation of *flowry* in the intricate image of 48, where also the kindred symbol of *light* or *seeing* and *night* or *darkness* is tied up with the flowry symbol. In stanza one, line 5,

> Sweet Babes . . . .
> The Bloomes of Martyrdome,

though *Bloomes* is a simple image, it is heavily laden with kindred connotations. *Smile* is another symbol of joy, and hence by the extension of the concept, of the gift and presence of heavenly radiance; as, by itself in 30 "(The fairest, and the first borne smile of Heav'n)," by extension through flowers in 3 and 14 "(These bright Flowers . . . They were the smiling sons of those sweet Bowers, That drinke the deaw of Life"; and, "Hee saw a vernall smile, sweetly disfigure Winters sad face)." Though the literal significances of the images in these passages still overwhelm the reader, and by their multiplicity and ingenuity wrap him in confusion, it is only in so far as the sensuousness has become an intellectual abstraction that the whole passage has meaning. The poetic communication of the whole is widely different from that of Marino.

Another notable quality of Crashaw's images as compared with those of Marino is his blending of the literal and the figurative, or of two figures from wholly different contexts. In stanza 19, lines 1 and 2,

> While thus Heav'ns highest counsails, by the low
> Footsteps of their Effects, hee trac'd too well

and in 56, with its *Engines on tiptoe in their Braynes*, the effect seems the product of wilful ingenuity working upon a total lack of a sense of humor. In 41 it appears to spring from the desire for intensity. In 8, the blend forces the whole passage to take on a certain abstraction which is akin to Crashaw's symbolism.

> His flaming Eyes dire exhalation,
> Vnto a dreadful pile gives fiery Breath;
> Whose unconsum'd consumption preys upon
> The never-dying Life, of a long Death.
> In this sad House of slow Destruction,
> (His shop of flames) hee fryes himselfe, beneath
> A mass of woes, his Teeth for Torment gnash,
> While his steele sides sound with his Tayles long lash.

> (Che la vista pestifera, e sanguigna,
> Con l'alito crudel, ch'avampa e fuma,
> La pira accende horribile, e maligna,
> Che 'nconsumabilmente altrui consuma,
> Con amaro stridor batte, e digrigna
> I denti aspri di rugine, e di schiuma;
> E de' membri d'acciaio entro le fiamme
> Fà con l'estremo suo sonar le squamme.)[13]

Whether we read the stanza in itself or compare it with its original, two things strike us: the concentration and imaginative intensity in lines 3-5; and the clattering confusion of the mixed and incongruous images of the next two lines. From the grandiose suggestiveness of the first lines, we drop suddenly into the confined precision of the *shop* of flames and thence to the grotesque cooking place, with its strange fuel. It is not merely the blending of literal and figurative that is ludicrous. But all the insistent and literal associations of *shop* give it a connotation destructive of the emotion created in the first three lines; and to any direct sensuous perception such as is present in the reader in his uninitiate state, these connotations are still dominant. Yet Crashaw uses the image as if the literal connotations did not exist; he abstracts it to the value of its symbolic connotations of mean and petty toil, of material and bourgeois worldliness, set against the idea of spiritual being. *Shop* in 37, line 3, *Hell's shop of slaughter*, carries the same connotation of the trivial and evil. Indeed the symbolic connotation depends for its meaning just on the mean limitations of

[13] That the glance of his eyes, pestilential and bloody, with his cruel breath, that flares and smokes, enkindles the pile horrible and malign, which unconsumable, consumes others, with bitter shrieking he strikes and gnashes his teeth sharp with rust and foam; and between the flames he makes the scales of his steel limbs resound with his tail.

the literal association, that is to say, on the primary sense experience of Crashaw and ourselves, and on the shock of the contrast; but though the literal meaning has these limiting connotations the symbolic meaning as it is abstracted from the literal is itself grandiose. In this way, I think, such a passage grew in Crashaw's imagination. However much he is led on by a superficial habit of style and play of wit, he himself as an artist strives at the most intense moments of the poem to distill unified thought and spiritual meaning out of the scattered facts and sensations that shroud them; though he has hardly succeeded in conveying his own experience to the reader. And certainly Humpty-Dumpty could fairly have maintained that Crashaw owed his words much over-time pay on Saturday evening. But in later developments, in his last poems, he reaches often the realization here denied him and us.

In Crashaw's metaphors and elaborations as compared with his original in Marino, there exist, then, side by side, two distinct modes, the first seeking abundant sensuousness in picture and sound, and the delight arising from picture and sound, the other abstracting the sensuousness of particular experience from the concrete and yet leaving it actual. The first seeks through the sensuous, as Spenser sought, to suggest moral sentiment; the second, by creating a language of ideas that is still vivid with all the realities of momentary being, seeks to create organized consciousness that is not an abstraction from experience, but a synthesis of it; thought as experience and not as analysis. Thus the two modes of Spenserianism and symbolism at their best have a common impulse.

So far, we have sought to get at Crashaw's style through a comparison of change in detail from his original. But more significant than any detailed changes which Crashaw made in Marino's poem are the changes in interpretation. Marino's poem expresses the conventional significance of its story as dryly as it may. Crashaw's is charged in every line with the burden of its meaning; the struggle between infinite destroying malice and infinite saving love, between life and death, is present in almost every line.

One of the characteristics of the ingenious Marinistic style, as of the style of the neo-Latin religious epigrammatists and elegists, is its definition by contrasts. Marino does not miss the rhetorical opportunities offered by his present theme. The opening line trumpets the contrast of theme between this and his former work; in stanza 8, contrast adds a touch of real moral horror to the dragon terrors of Satan; 14 and 15 depend on a contrast of verdure and barrenness, shade and light, which marks Satan's vision of the Nativity; 22, 23, and 65 take up the traditional theme of the descent of Godhead into an infant human form; 27 and 29 the radiance of Heaven and the darkness of Hell; 66 defines in highly rhetorical images the contrast between Herod's state and power and the poverty of the infant Christ. Crashaw not only makes most of these contrasts more elaborate than they are in the original, but he insists upon their moral meaning, often intensifying the contrast to paradox. Marino creates physical melodrama, Crashaw the ironic paradox between the physical order and the real order of the world. Moreover Crashaw develops such contrast, in which for him lies the essential meaning of the story, at points where it is not suggested by his original. For instance, in Marino the *argomento* is a simple summary of the action whereas Crashaw's argument is both highly paradoxical and allusive. In the eighth stanza, Marino's *Inconsumabilmente altrui consuma* suggests to Crashaw the intensely imaginative lines we have already looked at. The bare contrast of his

> Vede de la felice santa notte
> Le tacit' ombre, e i tenebrosi horrori
> De la voce del Ciel percosse, e rotte,
> E vinti da gli angelici splendori,[14]

gives rise to,

> Hee saw how in that blest Day-bearing Night,
> The Heav'n-rebuked shades made hast away;
> How bright a Dawne of Angels with new Light
> Amaz'd the midnight world, and made a Day
> Of which the Morning knew not.

In 22, taking up the whole contrast delineated by Marino, Crashaw wrings out the last bit of ingenious figure that is verbally sug-

[14] He saw the silent shadows and the dark horrors of the happy, holy night, struck and broken by the voice of Heaven, and conquered by the angelic splendors.

gested; but with ingenuity he gains also a new reality. As a last example we may note the seventh line of the twenty-third stanza,

> Che la gloria a soffrir venga gli affanni[15]

to see how the conventionally impressive statement of Marino in Crashaw bursts into imaginative life and gathers up for us in one moment the theme of the sacrifice:

> That Glories selfe should serve our Griefs, & feares.

Throughout, Crashaw explicitly defines sentiment and moral precept, the meaning of every situation and of every analogy. Again, to illustrate is to be tempted to quote the whole poem. The line already quoted from stanza 21 in another connection shows the intensifying of the sentiment, where

> E che vestita
> Gir di spoglia mortal deggia la vita[16]

becomes

> And life it selfe wear Deaths fraile Livery.

The change to the word *impartiall* in stanza 40, line 7,

> Swinging a hugh Sith stands impartiall *Death*
> (La gran falce rotar morte superba)

is a beautiful example of Crashaw's power of making the particular moment realize a larger truth. Stanzas 52 and 53 give examples of very explicit sentiment. This explicit insistence on meaning is responsible for some of the grotesque imagery, in which, pivoting on some literal external detail, Crashaw tries to wrench it to spiritual meaning, as in the first stanza.

> O be a Dore
> Of language to my infant Lips, yee best
> Of Confessours: whose Throates answering his swords,
> Gave forth your Blood for breath, spoke soules for words.

All the passage beginning in stanza 25 in which Satan contemplates his fallen state is full of this rich allusiveness and concentration of meaning, and must have been often read by Milton.

---

[15] That Glory came to suffer woes.
[16] And that life should go clad in mortal spoils.

Crashaw's poem, then, is not only much richer and more concrete than Marino's. It is more repellant in part than Marino because in a measure beyond Marino's poem it is stiff with ingenious and trivial figure. But, and this is the signal difference from Marino, working up through the fantastic rhetoric is an intensity of concern that transmutes ingenuity into symbolic expression and fills almost every part with the meaning of the whole.[17]

In comparing the two poems thus closely, we find that, though Crashaw follows Marino thought by thought, his most ingenious images are not in his original. And we have already suggested why *La Strage* is not typical of Marino's style. Hence to realize to the full the direct influence of Marinism on Crashaw, we must look at other poems. As Mr. Martin and Signor Praz point out, there are also a lyric and several epigrams translated from Marino. The Latin epigram, Act. 7.16. *Ad Judaeos Mactatores Stephani* is a close translation of four lines from Marino's *Nel Martiro di S. Stefano*, lines characterized by their scholastic analysis. Crashaw's lines are, however, dramatized beyond Marino's into the more set rhetoric of the epigram. Here he seems to draw from Marino what Marino had in common with the neo-Latin epigram. The Latin epigram *In vulnera pendentis Dom.* with its English adaptation, *On the wounds of our crucified Lord* is developed from an image of Marino's and the lyric verse, *On our Crucified Lord, naked and bloody*, translates another figure of four lines from one of Marino's sonnets,

> Suda sangue (ahi bontade)
> Re, che prendendo la corona, e'l regno,
> Di rugiadoso porpora celeste
> Tesse a la membra sue la regia veste.[18]

In this image, Marino pivots on the inessential physical fact that both garments and in this case blood cover a body, working it up into a meretricious dramatic contrast. Crashaw keeps the

---

[17] In power to illuminate the parts with the sense of the whole, and in grandeur of feeling, this translation of Crashaw's from Marino should be compared with another English adaptation from an Italian source, Robert Southwell's adaptation of Tansillo's *Lagrime di S. Pietro*, which has something of the same diffusion of meaning through the whole. The relation of Southwell's poem to its source is described and discussed by Signor Praz in "Robert Southwell's 'St Peter's Complaint' and its sources." *Modern Language Review.* Vol. XIX (1926) pp. 273-90.

[18] He sweated blood (ah goodness) he the King, who, taking the crown and the kingdom, wove for his limbs the royal garment of blooming celestial purple.

pivot, but turns the labored pseudo-syllogism of Marino into a flash of insight that almost renders it poetry,

> Thee with thyself they have too richly clad,
> Opening the purple wardrobe of thy side.

The Latin epigram from Marino keeps the same syllogistic form as its original. In the English lyric version of the Latin, the image is developed even more intricately than its original, but at the same time it is both more compressed and more lush. It can hardly be said on that account to be the more successful. For in this field of the physical detail of the Passion, perhaps the less fully realized in poetic detail the better. The important fact to note is that both poems depend upon Marino for the logical basis of their image, and both English poems transform the nature of that image by floriation and by swiftness of intuition. In the former fact, both show the Marinistic influence on the imagery of Crashaw and hence indicate that influence on the *Sospetto* even where Crashaw in that poem is not translating from anything specific in his original,—for both epigrams resemble the imagery of that poem—and in the latter fact, both show the same transmuting ardor as the *Sospetto.*

The lyric, *Out of the Italian,* "Love now no fire hath left him," comes from Marino's madrigal *Foco d'Amore diuiso,*

> Amor non hà più foco,
> Che'l divise frà noi;
> Diede l'arsura à me, la luce à voi . . . . .[19]

This kind of Alexandrian conceit depends for its force on the lucid and unadorned demonstration of the proposition and on the contrapuntal verbal and sound play. Crashaw follows the steps of the demonstration as Marino states it, but he obscures it and dissolves the force of its logic by excessive picturization of detail,

> The heat commanding in my *Heart* doth sit . . . .
> . . . . in mutuall Names
> Of Love, burne both together.

In the last phrase he gives a momentary glamorous illusion of mysterious meaning, but sacrifices the social tone of semi-comic sentiment that is the point of Marino's poem. He also loses form.

[19] Love has no longer any fire, for he has divided it between us: he has given the heat to me, the light to you.

*The Weeper* and *The Teare*, as Mr. Martin points out, derive most directly from the epigrams of Franciscus Remondus, with hints from Cabilliavus and from Herman Hugo, and with a very few specific imitations from Marino. Remond and Cabilliau treat the specific theme of Mary Magdalen's tears for the death of Christ; Marino wrote a number of poems on Mary Magdalen. Of the general growth of the Magdalen theme in the epigrammatists and in Italian poetry and art Signor Praz gives a brilliant definition in his book already referred to, concluding that the Magdalen, in this art, has the affliction of repentance and no religion.[20] Still there is a marked difference between the Italian poet and the Jesuits. For in the former, the development remains one of pure aesthetic or witty play, but the treatments of the story by the Jesuits, despite surface concentration on ingenious imagery, sharp antitheses, and paradoxes, belong to the fringe of the contemplative exercise and dwell upon religious meaning. For instance, while the epigram of Remond uses an ingenious comparison of the Golden Pactolus,

> Si amanare oculis posset Pactolus ab istis
> Aurifer hac iret ditior amnis aqua,[21]

it is in order to stress the idea. He uses golden as a type of the precious in a manner ultimately descended from the Book of Revelation, whereas Marino's gold and pearls, in *Per la Maddelena alla Croce* or in stanzas 6 and 7 of *La Maddelena Ai Piedi Di Cristo*, come from the neck of a Neopolitan beauty. The whole essential difference of spirit is manifest in a brief passage. Stanza 14 of Crashaw's poem depends both upon the lines cited from Remond and upon these from the second of Marino's poems,

> Dalla testa e da' lumi
> e di chiome e di lagrime confonde,
> sparse in lucide stille e'n tepid' onde
> costei, torrenti e fiumi.
> Oh richezza, oh tesoro!
> Due piogge: una d'argento e l'altra d' oro.[22]

which mingle to become,

---

[20] *Op. cit.*, chapter xvii, p. 238.

[21] If Pactolus could flow from these eyes, his gold-bearing stream would go richer with this water.

[22] From her head and from her eyes, hair and tears mingled together, spread in lucid drops and in warm waters these, torrents and streams. Oh richness, oh treasure! two showers: one of silver, the other of gold.

Golden though hee bee,
Golden *Tagus* murmurs though,
Might hee flow from thee
Content and quiet would he goe,
Richer far does he esteeme
Thy silver, then his golden streame.[23]

The sensuously rich color of Marino has been added to the thought of Remond, but the sensuousness has become symbolic, and at the same time the whole is personalized by something of Elizabethan ardor and given dramatic reality by something of Crashaw's special power of attaching us by the end of a cobweb to the sky.

The specific imitations of Marino in *The Weeper*, however, do not give the full measure of Marino's influence upon the two poems *The Weeper* and *The Teare*. To grasp this influence we must turn to Marino's religious verse on other themes. Of all religious themes treated in Italian poetry, the Magdalen theme seems the one most specifically taken over with the full connotation of its Pagan and sensuous origin. As J. A. Symonds points out, when the Christian theme replaced the Pagan in art, St. Sebastian replaced Apollo as the type of masculine beauty, and it is the beauty of his nude form rather than the signs of his martyrdom that forms the central interest in pictures of him. In the same way Mary Magdalen replaced Venus, the very type of surrender to the beauty of the senses; and from art into poetry she came bringing her context with her. Bringing, too, for a self-conscious age, the fussiness of manner that springs from insincere division of purpose. Hence in the Magdalen poems we expect to find and do find a sensuality greater than that in the other religious poems of Marino. When he writes of the Passion, in him, as in the religious verse of others, another type of sensuous and luscious image comes in, the imagery of the *Song of Songs,* that grand source, as has often been noted, especially when taken allegorically, of the tasteless and unrestrained in poetry;—and this imagery comes in not controlled by feeling as in the original; and since it is not so controlled, it is conventionalized and coarsened. But this imagery, unlike the sensuous Magdalen imagery, which is used with direct physical intent, is used with formal

---

[23] In the revised version, stanza xii; slightly altered from the original form, but not in any detail affecting our comparison.

meaning, and handled with fantastic and purely formal development both of the image itself and of the antithetic analysis.

> Vscite, Vscite a rimirar pietose
> Schiere del Paradiso cittadine
> Il vostro Re schernito; e qual su 'l crine
> Novo, e stranio diadema Amor gli pose:
> De le tempie trafitte, e sanguinose
> Il vivo humor de la purpuree brine
> Voi rasciugate; e da l'acute spine
> Venite a cor le già cadente rose.
> E voi, felici voi, s'una di quelle
> Punte, ch'al Re del Ciel passan la testa
> Sentirete in voi stesse, anime belle,
> Ben potrai tu mio cor, cinto di questa,
> La corona sprezzar, che 'l Ciel di stelle,
> E che di raggi il Sol porta contesta.[24]

In other religious poems where there is neither of these traditions, the purely ingenious image is common; the image depending, as we have said, on no emotional harmony or descriptive interpretation of its object, but on the wit's perception of a literal and extraneous resemblance in circumstance or physical detail between image and subject, or upon some analysis of doctrine, using these physical resemblances as the geometrician uses his symbols. Thus since the Virgin is the child of God, she becomes,

> Figlia di Dio, chę da l'eterne mente
> Santa e vera Minerua, a guerra uscita . . . .[25]

His fantastic resemblances Marino has to some extent in common with the epigrammatists; the extreme exaggeration of them and the grouping of them in an unanalytical series is his own. The epigrammatists seek to make everything in this world indiscriminately and incongruously a chart of the other; Marino, on the contrary, to whom all things have become jaded by loss of meaning, all things remaining only things, strives to refresh them by change of physical aspect. In such images two types of develop-

[24] Come forth, come forth pious throngs of citizens of Paradise, to gaze upon your King, scorned; and see what a new and strange diadem Love has placed upon his hair; wipe from his pierced and bloody temples the living fluid of the purple; and come pluck the already falling roses from the sharp thorns. And you, happy you, if you feel in yourselves one of those points that pierced the head of the King of Heaven, fair spirits! well mayst thou, my heart, crowned with this, scorn the crown which the Heaven wears woven of stars, the Sun of rays.

[25] Daughter of God, who, a holy and true Minerva, from the eternal mind comest forth to war.

ment are common; either the prolonged demonstration of the physical analogy and the doctrine that may be demonstrated in it, or the rapid series of shocks of wit. The former appealed more to a mind like Donne's than to Crashaw's, and did not much influence Crashaw. The latter, stepping us up, as it were, in a series of rapid steps to a kind of ecstasy, meant more to him. Two characteristic examples will illustrate this style in Marino.

Al Piaghe de San Franceso d'Ascese

Piaghe non son ma Stelle,
Stelle no, ma fiamelle
Di FRANCESCO le piaghe, e quel divino
Sangue, cui non pareggia Ostro, o Rubino,
Sangue none, ma foco, e vivi ardore:
Pero, ch'ei nutre al core
Sotto il cenere oscuro, onde si reste,
Serafino terien, fiamma celeste.[26]

Le Stelle

Or l' ingegno e le rime
a voi rivolgo, o stelle,
luci del ciel sublime,
tremule fiamme e belle,
de l'esequie del dí chiare facelle;
amorose faville
del primo foco ardente,
luminose scintille
del sommo Sol lucente,
raggi del bel de l'increata mente, . . .
sacre lampe dorate,
che i palchi eccelsi ed ampi
del firmamento ornate;
fochi innoceni e lampi
de' tranquilli de l'aria aperti campi; . . .
fiori immortali e nati
ne le campagne amene
de' sempiterni prati,
de le piagge serene
del ciel gemme minute, aurate arene;
danzatrici leggiadre. . . . . . . . . .[27]

[26] Wounds are they not. but Stars, not stars, but flames, the wounds of Francis, and that divine blood, which not Purple nor Ruby equals, not blood but flame, and living fire: for at the heart under the dark dust where they rest, they are nourished by a terrestrial seraph, a celestial flame.

[27] Now I turn my craft and my rhymes to you, o stars. sublime lights of heaven, quivering and fair flames, clear torches of the obsequies of a day; amorous sparks of the first burning fire, luminous sparkles of the supreme shining Sun, rays of the beauty of the uncreated mind, . . . sacred golden lamps, that decorate the great and lofty floor of the firmament; innocent fires and lamps of the tranquil open fields of the air, . . . flowers immortal born in the pleasant meadows of the eternal fields, tiny gems of the calm shores of heaven, golden sands; charming dancers, . . .

We have already seen in the epigrams that Crashaw derived from Marino traces of this type of imagery. *The Weeper* and *The Teare* are full of it. The first stanzas of the former are ample and crowded illustration.

> Haile *Sister Springs,*
> Parents of Silver-forded rills.
> Ever bubling things!
> *Thawing Christall! Snowy Hills!* . . .

The fourth stanza derives from Herman Hugo, but only a reader of Marino could have exaggerated it into the grotesque physicality of the third and fourth lines,

> Vpwards thou dost weepe,
> Heavens bosome drinks the gentle streame.
> Where th' milky rivers meet,
> Thine Crawles above and is the Creame.

Thus, though so little in these two poems has its actual source in Marino, they are preeminently Marinistic.

But the imagery is not merely Marinistic. The second stanza shows this well.

> Heavens thy faire Eyes bee,
> Heavens of ever-falling stars,
> Tis seed-time still with thee
> And stars thou sow'st whose harvest dares
> Promise the earth; to countershine
> What ever makes Heavens fore-head fine.

To call the tears stars because they are many and shining is Marinistic; and Marino might well have called the stars seeds because of the multiplicity with which they lie scattered in the sky. But the inextricable mixing of the two images, or the double aspect of the image of starry brilliance and multiplicity would have been impossible either to his clarity or to his mere wit. It is possible only where the images are names not for concrete realities, but, if one may so define it, for concrete sentiments; when they are two-thirds symbol; and when the whole is subdued from a process of intellection to an imaginative flash of light however obscured by fog. The choice of the verb *dares* in this context is typical of the poetry of emotional excitation, and not that of wit. Crashaw sacrifices clarity and taste, but he hovers on the verge of an ecstasy of concern. Not in the passage just cited but at its richest the imagery of *The Weeper* is like that of the *Sospetto*. One finds in it some of the special images repeated, the same pictorial richness and sentiment, the same compression. In these poems, then, Marino has supplied the rhetorical forms of the images—and *The Weeper* is so much a rhetorical *tour de force* that its rhetorical forms control its tone—but he has not supplied the shaping spirit. The same thing is true in a lesser degree of the *Sospetto*, which also has in the forms of the images much more of Marinism than was derived merely from its specific source, *La Strage*. In this poem, however, Crashaw's own temper prevails over the forms much more fully than in the Magdalen poems.

One other poem of Crashaw's shows specific indebtedness to Marino. It has never, I think, been pointed out that Crashaw's paraphrase of the mediaeval *Stabat Mater* probably owes something to Marino's poem upon that theme.[28] Marino's *Stabat Mater* is based upon the first four stanzas of the hymn, that description of the Virgin which in the Latin hymn precedes the plea of the singer to be made one with Christ's suffering. Now the mediaeval Latin hymns are at all moments full of their meaning. In them, where the figures of the story are personalized, as in these stanzas, it is only in order that we may be reminded how the great types of our daily human experience are doors to the meaning of the divine story. And in this particular hymn the treatment of the figure is left universal, with that perfect equilibrium between general interpretation and individual picture which, while it makes our private emotions illuminate the theme, yet never reduces its subject to the level of the particular person, and which hence is never remotely physical. In Marino, in handling such religious themes, that insistence on physical detail which is tasteless even in the lyric of earthly love is brought to the description of religious figures, to the destruction both of sublimity and of feeling. For feeling is dissipated in surface sensations as a blow shatters the magnetized energy of a steel rod. This detail of Marino's, dried up when its sentiment is divorced from actual experience and made the play of mere wit, is then drawn out in patterns of ingenuity such as are common in Marino. I see thee languish, with only vinegar to assuage thy thirst:

[28] Drummond of Hawthornden had already translated Marino's poem; but his version was unpublished and can hardly have been known to Crashaw.

Ne pur mi lice offrir ti
Pria, ch'n te Morte avara
Lo strale ultimo scocchi
Qual dele poppe gia, l'urne degli occhi.[29]

In the same way dramatic emotions are personalized and likewise tortured through all the ingenuities that wit can suggest, and experience never knew. Of such elements is the principal stuff of Marino's *Stabat Mater.* Crashaw's hymn, *Sancta Maria Dolorum,* unlike Marino's, develops the whole theme of Jacapone da Tode's hymn, the cry of the soul to win from contemplation of the Passion an anguish that may soften and save it. Like the mediaeval hymn, it palpitates with its own meaning; but it is totally unlike the simplicity of the *Stabat Mater,* and is, indeed, as Crashaw calls it, a descant upon that plain song, as a comparison of passages from each will show.

Fac me tecum piê fiere,
Crucifixo condolere
    Donec ego vixero;
Juxta crucem tecum stare
Et me tibi sociare
    In planctu desidero.

Virgo virginum praeclara,
Mihi jam non sis amara,
    Fac me tecum plangere.
Fac ut portem Çhristi mortem,
Passionis fac consọrtem
    Et plagas recolere.

Fac me plagis vulnerari,
Fac me cruce inebriari
    Et cruore Filii.
Flammis ne urar succensus,
Per te, Virgo, sim defensus
    In die judicii.

O Mother turtle-doue!
Soft sourse of loue
That these dry lidds might borrow
Something from thy full Seas of sorrow!
O in that brest
Of thine (the noblest nest

[29] Nor can I offer thee before greedy Death strike into thee his last dart, as formerly the vessels of my breasts, the vessels of my eyes.

Both of loue's fires & flouds) might I recline
This hard, cold, Heart of mine!
The chill lump would relent, & proue
Soft subject for the seige of loue.

O teach those wounds to bleed
In me; me, so to read
This book of loues, thus writ
In lines of death, my life may coppy it
With loyall cares.
O let me, here, claim shares;
Yeild somthing in thy sad praerogatiue
(Great Queen of greifes) & giue
Me too my teares; who though all stone,
Think much that thou shouldst mourn alone.

Yea let my life & me,
Fix here with thee,
And at the Humble foot
Of this fair TREE take our eternall root.
That so we may
At least be in loues way;
And in these chast warres while the wing'd wounds flee
So fast 'twixt him & thee,
My breast may catch the kisse of some kind dart,
Though as at second hand, from either heart.

O you. your own best Darts
Dear, dolefull hearts!
Hail; & strike home & make me see
That wounded bosomes their own weapons be . . .

The method here in Crashaw is that of the symbolism of the *Sospetto,* but exaggerated by the lyric theme. The passages in which Crashaw departs farthest from his source are those of the description of the Virgin's sorrow. They are also those in which he departs farthest from feeling and into the debased dialectic rhetoric of the passions. And in these passages there are very marked resemblances both in general concept and in specific images to Marino's version. This is plain in a comparison of Crashaw's stanza 1 with 7 of Marino,

Quanti del caro ogetto
Venian pietosi sguardi,
Tanti pungenti dardi
Le passavano il petto,

Con duol non meno atroce
Di quel, che'l Figlio tormentaua in Croce.[30]

In the shade of death's sad TREE
Stood dolefull SHEE.
Ah SHE! now by none other
Name to be known, alas, but SORROW'S MOTHER.
Before her eyes
Her's & the whole world's ioyes,
Hanging all torn she sees; and in his woes
And Paines, her Pangs & throes.
Each wound of His, from euery Part,
All, more at home in her owne heart.

And in the second and third of Crashaw as compared with the fifth and sixth of Marino.

Di qualunque scorgea
Tormento in lui piu graue,
Fatto vn fascio soaue
Intorno al cor s'havea
E pallidetta essangue
Spargea per l'altrui piaghe il proprio sangue.

Se tempia à lui, se palma
Pungeua ò chiodo ò spina,
Sentiasí la meschina
Da lor traffiger l'alma:
E spesso una ferita
In vn corpo offendea più d'una vita.[31]

What kind of marble than
Is that cold man
Who can look on & see,
Nor keep such noble sorrowes company?
Sure eu'en from you
(My Flints) some drops are due
To see so many vnkind swords contest
So fast for one soft Brest.
While with a faithfull, mutuall, floud
Her eyes bleed TEARES, his wounds weep BLOOD.

O costly intercourse
Of deaths, & worse,

[30] As many pitiable looks as came from the dear object, so many sharp darts passed into her chest, with grief not less cruel than that which tormented her Son on the Cross.

[31] Of whatever torments she saw in him more heavy, she had made a sweet band within at her heart and a bloodless paleness shed her own blood through the wounds of the other. If nail or thorn pricked his temple or his palm, the wretched creature felt her soul transfixed therewith: and often a wound in a body injuries more than one life.

Diuided loues. While son & mother
Discourse alternate wounds to one another;
Quick Deaths that grow
And gather, as they come & goe:
His Nailes write swords in her, which soon her heart
Pays back, with more then their own smart
Her *Swords*, still growing with his pain,
Turn Speares, & straight come home again.

In these and a few other stanzas, 4, 7, and 8, Crashaw owes Marino much, not only of the rhetorical forms of the images, but of the rhetorical types of the passions. The essential feeling, however, and the essential poetic method of the two poems are wholly different.

The same relationship is true in a lesser and more general way of other of Crashaw's religious verse. *On the bleeding wounds of our crucified Lord* throws some of the wild Marinistic patterns across a theme which was suggested to Crashaw, probably, by the contemplations of Thomas à Kempis or Madre Teresa; and Marinistic rhetoric is present in the *Hymne of the Nativity;* rhetoric suggested both by Marinism in general and by specific poems on the Virgin and on the Nativity, though the poem as a whole is not Marinistic.

Marinism as it appears in Crashaw may be defined as including several aspects. First among these is the use of ingenious figures that depend upon resemblances of physical form or inessential circumstances in figure and subject, figures in which the comparison is developed for its own sake and does not either carry us forward to an analysis of the ideas involved in the subject, or illuminate the emotion. Then, secondly, Crashaw's Marinism is apparent in an insistence upon the physical detail of the subject, detail that is often trivial, with a resultant sensationalism. Finally, it is a schematic analysis of the emotions, using the dialectic of violent contrast, an analysis that gives the passions the same aridity as the concrete detail with which they are bound up. All this depends upon wit. At its keenest, the wit gives a pointedness of demonstration that may be very effective for the poetry of a slight world concerned chiefly to realize and control its feelings by a standard of social manners. But the detached keenness that is the charm of the social lyric or of the poem of sophisticated sentiment was totally alien to Crashaw. The dialectic, the ingenious figure, and the physicality wherewith that sentiment is shaped and voiced, however, influenced him deeply. They gave to much of his verse the rhetorical forms of the images, and in part the rhetorical forms of the passions.

These forms were animated in Crashaw, however, by a very different vision from that of Marino, and this vision in the end made of the physicality a symbolism and of the ingenuity, by and through this symbolism, a subtle analysis of meanings, an appeal from this world and its sensationalism to a world of emotions and of visions.

As we have seen, the Marinistic forms were not the only ones Crashaw used. The rhetorics and the epigrammatists played their part. And a very different force of expression, which we may best define as Spenserian manner and meaning, with fresh Elizabethan energy, gave play at the same time to another side of his nature, his sensuous radiance and spiritual feeling. As Crashaw's poetry developed its technique of expression, the Spenserian impulse yielded to the other forms. But even while these other modes were developing in him a style choked with ingenious, superficial, and often trivial metaphor, those deeper impulses and vision at work in him were energetic enough to enkindle imaginative and spiritualized life in the cold and artificial forms to which he had apprenticed himself. This life is fully apparent in his later poems.

Before, however, we consider his further development, we shall glance briefly at his other translations. They show in general the same traits as those already defined.

Most important of these are his English versions of his Latin epigrams. Either these are later than the Latin epigrams, or they show that, at the same time he was writing most of the Latin epigrams, Crashaw definitely considered another style than that of the Latin verse suited to poetry in the vernacular. This style is more floriate and more sensuous than that of the Latin epigram, and its more lyric feeling is sometimes represented, also, by lyric measure. It is also more explicit in its statement of its moral than its Latin originals; is more ingenious, and at the same time more colloquial. One or two examples will suffice to illustrate the difference.

*Ego sum ostium*

Jamque pates. cordisque seram gravis hasta reclusit,
Et clavi claves undique te reserant.
Ah, vereor, sihi ne manus impia clauserit illas,
Quae caeli has ausa est sic aperire fores.

*I am the Doore.*

And now th'art set wide ope, The Speare's sad Art,
Lo! hath unlockt thee at the very Heart:
Hee to, himselfe (I feare the worst)
And his owne hope
Hath *shut* these Doores of Heaven, that durst
Thus set them *ope.*

*Non solùm vinciri sed & mori paratus sum*

Non modò vincla, sed & mortem tibi, Christe, subibo,
Paulus ait, docti callidus arte doli.
Diceret hos aliter: Tibi non modò velle *ligari,*
Christe, sed & *solvi* nempe paratus ero.

*I am not ready onely to be bound but to dye.*

Come death, come bands, nor do you shrink, my eares,
At those hard words mans cowardise calls feares.
Save those of feare, no other bands feare I:
No other death then this; the feare to dye.

*On the wounds of our crucified Lord.* (O these wakefull wounds of thine!) develops its five stanzas of Marinistic lyric from an epigram of eight lines, and *Easter day* is even more highly elaborated in the most sensuous and complex manner of the *Sospetto.*

The lines from Vergil's *Georgics* show the same method applied even to the classical Latin author. And even the satire of Petronius and the epigram of Martial take, within their small compass, the same tone. Minor borrowings from the classic and silver Latin authors and from the neo-Latinists, abundantly cited in Mr. Martin's notes, need not detain us, for all are but exercises and all exhibit the same influences and the same traits. *Musicks Duell* and the *Alexias* elegies carry us again to Jesuit neo-Latin poetry; the former, one of Crashaw's most carefully wrought poems, the latter no more than an exercise, elaborating the formal reflections of its original in the spirit of the *Sospetto*, but without the living concreteness or the spiritual feeling which intensify and concentrate that poem. One line from the *Alexias* elegies may be cited to show how, unkindled by such a spirit, insistence on vivid but inorganic sense detail may destroy concreteness. The line of Remond, "Vulnerit (heu!) teneros quo vagas orbe pedes" Crashaw translates "In what strange path my lord's fair footsteppes bleed," losing the imaginative realization and the pathos of the original. In *Musicks Duell* Crashaw surrendered fully to all that he could do with the delights of the senses. It is much more rich in sentiment than the poem of Strada from which it is taken, and also in natural magic,—(Most divine service) whose so early lay, *Prevents the Eye-lidds of the blushing day*." All the drama of the picture, all the exquisitely delicate description of the varying shades of musical mood, all the subtle and enraptured description of musical ecstasy are Crashaw's own. Its richness in the reproduction of sound might owe a little to such a poem as *La Cantatrice, a Settimia, figliuola di Guilio Romano,* by the Marinisto, Tamoso Stigliani, but its mingled Spenserianism and ingenuity brought to sensuous life are pure Crashaw. We have no means of knowing whether Crashaw had read any of the poetry of the Marinisti. There is no specific evidence in his work of familiarity with them, and this analogue in the treatment of music is the only instance I know which suggests comparison.

The translation of the opening of the *Christus Patiens* of Grotius shows, in contrast to the severely compressed and plain style of its original, the type of richness found in the *Sospetto*, and marks that as the author's distinctive style. There are many instances of extreme ingenuity in the Marinistic manner, but the verses as a whole are marked by the individual poetic spirit Crashaw had developed for himself, and despite the frivolous detail on their surface they show a grand sense of the chiaroscuro of their theme and something of that centrality and thought-burdened allusiveness which in the greatest parts of the *Sospetto* remind us of Milton.

The translations as a whole mark a step in an aesthetic pilgrimage as deliberate and as dramatic as anything in Crashaw's intellectual or spiritual history. And to us who read these particular poems of Crashaw's with Elizabethan poetry before them and

Milton to follow, it cannot but seem a wayward step. For they comprehend passages of the worst taste, not merely in rhetoric but in spirit, perhaps to be found in the whole range of English poetry,—the most distinctively Marinistic passages; and at the same time they comprehend gleams of a noble, ardent, and intense vision, and moments of rich, magical, and fluid expression which show what Crashaw could do when free of Marinism. Why Crashaw's course took him far apart from Jacobean classicism it is easy to see. But why did he turn his back upon the Elizabethan tradition, and why did he condemn his vision to narrow itself to the task of enspiriting Marinism? In part, we may say of Crashaw in common with others who imitated Marino that he did so simply under the pressure of a mere poetic fashion in its turn replacing Petrarchism, especially as the growth of sophistication put a premium upon ingenuity. And this fashion prevailed the more readily because it was also related in more profoundly intellectual natures to a renewed and altered growth of dialectic, and to a rise of rationalism as well as to a subtilizing of the sensibilities. But Crashaw had, moreover, already advanced some way in this direction before he studied Marino; for he had already in his epigrams—and in the epigram Crashaw had done more serious and significant work than other poets—developed something of a serious aesthetic form based upon highly dialectic patterns of thought, and at the same time on melodramatic rhetoric. Moreover, Marinism was not an isolated phenomenon in literature; there was a large continental activity in this field of dialectic poetry, as we may call it; and it was as natural that a poet of such interests as Crashaw should turn to contemporary continental models of religious decoration as that English devotional prose writers a generation before, in the absence of a current English tradition, should have raided continental devotional treatises. There could be no permanent turning back for Crashaw to the poetic method of Spenser, as there could be no turning back to his religious and moral outlook, to his integration of life. For good or ill, all the intellectual endeavor summed up in Bacon, all the connotations, all the sharpening and twisting and limitation of definitions involved in the Puritan controversy lay between them, and it was natural that Crashaw should look to the continuing tradition of the continent and to the Counter-Reformation,—to Marino and the neo-Latinists—in these minor and sometimes trivial literary forms, just as we know that he was ultimately to find his way to peace in the realm of deeper religious feeling through the inspiration of the profounder manifestations of that movement in St. Teresa. We may remind ourselves, too, how on the continent, in St. Teresa literature, the very minor forms were connected with the greater movement.

Moreover, as it seemed to us in our study of Crashaw's life, there was much of sensationalism in Crashaw's first imaginative unfolding. This sensationalism found a sympathetic stimulus in Marino; and at the same time Crashaw's intellectual temper, which had already been molded to the forms of thought of the epigrams, found a congenial counterpart to his sensationalism in the ingenuity of Marino and in the neo-Latins. But had these latter not shown him their ingenuity bent to the riddling of religious meanings, he would not, I think, have tried to forge this whole literature into the chief instrument of expression for his deepening religious feeling.

The story of Crashaw's inner history is the story of his effort to organize his sensationalism with relation to an ever-growing centre and in so organizing it to idealize and sublimate it. For Crashaw accepted his fundamental philosophical ground seemingly without conflict, and an intellectual struggle does not form part of his growth. At the time he was making these translations, he was moving into the Laudian position in theology, and he was concentrating more and more upon his contemplative vocation. And this devotion to contemplation is the spring of energy that transformed Marinism and forced that trivial, alien, and sensational form to bear a deeper poetry, which Crashaw could no longer express with satisfaction to himself in the great channel opened by Spenser. We shall see in our next chapter the final development of the symbolism to which, instead, he turned.

## Chapter V

# EMBLEM AND *IMPRESA*: THE MATURING OF CRASHAW'S IMAGERY

We have already suggested in our comparison of Crashaw's *Sospetto* with Marino's poem the direction of the impulses and the nature of the vision which enabled Crashaw to kindle to poetic life the artificial forms springing from the study of rhetoric and from Marino. But much as this spirit depended for its growth on Crashaw's own inner growth, and highly individual as his work became, he did not advance alone here any more than in his earlier technical studies. Just as the school of rhetoricians and poetical craftsmen had developed the technique of the ingenious metaphor, so another school of craftsmen had been studying how to turn ingenious wit to the use of quickened meanings. These were the emblematists, the makers of *imprese*, the designers of allegorical tapestry. As we have already said when we spoke of Crashaw's reading, his study of emblems cannot be referred to a distinct stage in his development; but as we shall see in the course of this chapter, emblematic figures appear in his translations from Marino and are woven through and through the texture of his hymns. Thus we may link the emblematic mode of thought in him with the deepening of his religious vocation and with his concentration as an artist upon religious themes.

Some specific indebtedness of Crashaw to the emblematists has already been pointed out by Mr. L. C. Martin, by Mr. H. J. C. Grierson, and by Signor Praz.[1] It is very likely that he knew *Af-beeldinghe van d'eerste eeuwe der Societyt Iesu. . . .* T'Antwerpen . . . M.DC.XL;[2] and it is certain that he was familiar with Hugo's *Pia Desideria,* the drawings of which were later used by Quarles in his volumes of Emblems, and that he knew such emblematic drawings (largely Dutch) as were used to illustrate the Little Gidding Concordances. It is unlikely that this list

[1] See the notes to Mr. Martin's edition of the *Poems.*
[2] Signor Praz, quoted in Martin, note to page 236, p. 446.

exhausts the number of emblem books known to him, for this form of art and literature was exceedingly popular both in England and on the continent. For instance, besides innumerable foreign editions from 1523 on, there were English editions of Alciatus alone in 1545, 1547, 1548 (3), 1549 (2), 1550 (2), 1557, to name the first ten, and countless others up through 1660.[3] And besides English editions of foreign collections, by 1634 England had produced Whitney's *Choice of Emblems,* 1556 (first published at Leyden by Plantin), with verses and emblems drawn largely from Paradin,[4] Abraham Fraunce's *Insignium* . . . , 1588, Peachum's collection, 1612, Quarles' *Emblems,* 1635, and several others not extant. The emblem, too, had a recognized place in the handbook of rhetoric, as in Buchler's digest of Pontanus, which contains a section on emblematic writing following the section on the epigram.

The emblems were the product, almost entirely, of religious and moral didacticism. On this side, they were deeply rooted in mediaeval fable, allegory, and symbolism, and in Renaissance development of the mediaeval theory that art had a two-fold function, to teach and to delight, a theory according to which poetry was composed of two elements; profitable subject matter (doctrina), theoretically supplied by allegory, and style.[5] Through this theory, verse and picture were often closely related as allegory and in picture as either interpretation or sensuous embodiment of that allegory; and as Miss Evans points out in her *Pattern,* at the same time that inscriptions of all kinds were often used to amplify or elucidate picture, decorative picture often existed simply to illustrate verbal allusion. For instance, a Flemish tapestry of the Perfections of Our Lady, given to Rheims Cathedral by Robert de Lenoncourt in 1530, pictures symbols of the perfections of the Virgin, interpreted by Latin inscriptions on banderoles: *Lilium inter spinas, Planctatio rose, Ortus conclusus, Virga Jesse,* and so on; and underneath runs the verse:

> Marie vierge chaste, de mer estoille,
> Porte du ciel, comme soleil eslue,
> Puis de vive eaue, ainsi que lune belle,

[3] On the editions of Alciatus, see Henry Green, *Andrea Alciati and his Book of Emblems. A Biographical and Bibliographical Study.* (London, M.DCCC.LXXII.)

[4] On this book and on the dates of the other books of emblems, see Green's *On the Emblems of Geffrey Whitney, of Nantwich, of the Sixteenth Century. A paper read before the Architectural, Archeological and Historical Society of Chester.* (1865)

[5] Donald Leman Clark, *op. cit.,* p. 55. See also Spingarn's *A History of Literary Criticism in the Renaissance.* (New York: 1899).

Tour de David, lis de noble value,
Cité de Dieu, clair mirouer non pollue,
Cèdre exalté, distillante fontaine,
En ung jardin fermée, est rêsolue
De besongnier, et de si grace pleine.[6]

In parallel fashion, many of the emblems which fill emblem books are simply illustrations of fables which are told in the accompanying verse; others represent scenes from classical myth which are allegorically interpreted in the verse; and still others picture simply an allegorical figure which the verse interprets. An example of the first type is found in one of the emblems of Sambucus (the second emblem in the fourth edition). The epigraph reads, *In copia minor error*. The emblem represents a tree with a monkey in its branches, a man standing to one side of the tree, and on the other a fox looking up at the tree. It is thus interpreted:

Callida verrit humum longa vulpecule cauda,
Irrisit nimium simia ἄπωρ onus.
Subiicit at vulpes prolixè turpia malle
  Abdere, quàm nudas semper habere nates.
Caussa fuit melior vulpis: superesse quod ornat,
  Et prodest, satius quàm caruisse nimis.
Prodigus in vitio minus est, quam pròrsus auarus,
  Virtutis potiùs congruit ille modo.[7]

Then, too, many of Whitney's *Emblems* are mere illustrated fables, concluding their verse with the explicitly drawn moral which is characteristic of the fable; as for example *Temeritas*, which represents a chariot drawn by wild horses, the driver airily perched and obviously about to be thrown. Verse one explains that a waggoner is thrown if he be driven by fierce unknown horses, verse two, that the man who hath untamed affections, neglecting reason, falls headlong; and the whole concludes,

Then bridle will, and reason make thy guide,
So mayst thou stande, when others downe do slide.[8]

---

[6] *Pattern a Study of Ornament in Western Europe from 1180-1900.* (Oxford: MCM XXXI) Chapter III § 6, p. 148.
[7] *Emblemata et Aliquot Nummi Antiqui* Operis, Ioan. Sambvci Turnaviensis Pannonii. Quarta Editio. Cum emendatione & auctario Copioso ipsius auctoris. (Antverpiae, MDLXIV).
[8] *Whitney's "Choice of Emblems." A Facsimile Reprint.* Ed. Henry Green, (London, Chester, Nantwich, M. DCCC. LXVI.)

Good examples of classical mythology are Alciatus' *In Deo laetandum,* representing the rape of Ganymede, or his *Consilio, & virtute chimaeran superari, id est, fortiores & deceptores,* which represents Bellerophon slaying the Chimaera, with the verse,

> Bellerophon (vt fortis eques) superare chimaeron,
> Et Licij potuit sternere monstra sôli.
> Sic tu Pegaseis vectus petis aether a pennis:
> Consilioque animi monstra superba domas.[9]

The allegorical figure is represented in his *Sapientia humana, stultitia est apud Deum,* a reverend-headed old man with serpent's tail swimming in the sea; a figure which the verse interprets as follows:

> Quid dicam? quoniam hoc compellem nomine monstrum
> Biforme: quod non est homo nec est draco?
> Sed sine vir pedibus, summis sine partibus anguis,
> Vir anguipes dici, & homiceps anguis potest.
> Anguem pedit homo, hominem eructauit & anguis
> Nec finis hominis est, initium nec est ferae
> Sic olim Cecrops . . . .
> Haec vafrum est species, sed reeligione carentem,
> Terrena tantum quique, curet indicat.

But this graphic symbolism soon developed into an art of its own, flowering into its own complexity, the ancillary verse developing side by side with the pictures. And it will be noted of these emblem verses, as distinct from the allegorical, fabulous, or mythical types from which they derive, that emblem verses are more compressed, more allusive, and more ingenious than their originals. The fable seeks to make moral truths simple and apprehensible by representing them in terms of the familiar natural world; the myth seeks to personalize in typical and simplified form, as a character or a story, certain great forces and laws at work in the universe; it seeks to be simple that it may represent complex and intangible manifestations in their single essence; if it elaborates, it elaborates not its meaning but only the story which gives it sensuous life. It is only when myths are wrenched to Christian and moral meanings they were not formed to express that they become subtilized or ingenious. But in the emblem, the essential impressiveness and

[9] The numbers and paging of the emblems of Alciatus of course vary with the innumerable editions and are of no significance. The copy which happens to be available to me at the moment, and from which I quote, is a copy in the Public Library of New York City with title page missing, probably Roville 1551.

beauty were to lie in the allusiveness and the ingenuity, in the egg within egg of meaning nesting like a Chinese toy of art.

Indeed, we must not lose sight of the fact first that, though the emblem derives originally from literature, as Miss Evans reminds us, the verse became, in the first emblem books, purely ancillary; and of the second fact that, though the original verse was not always figurative, the emblem itself must, of its very nature, be ingeniously figurative and allusive, in as much as it sought to represent a whole moral principle visually within the compass of one small drawing. The symbol, representing one moral quality, may be simple; the emblem, seeking to represent a whole chapter of ethics in a word, must be ingenious and complex. The definition which Alciatus gives of the emblem stresses the virtues of ingenuity and allusiveness. And there is much significance, too, in the statement of Sambucus in his Preface *De Emblemate* that emblems must be select *like the notae of the Aegyptians and Pythagoreans*. Thus when fable, myth, and allegory passed from literary to plastic expression, they underwent very important changes, and thus it was the early emblems themselves, rather than emblem verse, which developed the artistic mode of ingenious figure directing its ingenuity to complex symbolism. Such figure, when developed in the art of drawing, was, by its nature, more complex than the ingenious image of the school of Marino, since it sought to be so much more comprehensive than the ingenuity which marks the Marinistic style and which was but a game of finding physical resemblances.

The verses, as we have seen, were not under the same compulsion. They might be simple. They had in common with the emblem they accompanied a moral purpose, and they might devote themselves solely to the enlargement of this moral leaving the delights of sensuousness and wit to the picture. Thus Whitney is naïvely simple, and thus Hugo used the emblem side by side with the long elegiac verses of his *Pia Desideria.* Yet, on the other hand, the subjects of the verse were the emblems themselves standing as a perpetual example to the writer; and too, it was natural that the imaginative approach which created the emblems should also influence the verse. This impetus might manifest itself, first, in the love of the condensed statement. And, as Henry Green showed, many of the emblems of Alciatus were from Greek originals in the epigrams. But at the same time, as the epigrammatic form reminds us, the emblem and the neo-Latin didactic epigram are the fruit of the same intellectual and moral impulse. Wherefore naturally these epigram verses have become in their ingenuity more like the other neo-Latin epigrams than like their Greek originals. The imaginative impulse which created the emblem might show itself, in the second place, in the verse, as well as in the picture, in ingenuity of figure. The following lines from the eighth elegy of the first book of Hugo's *Pia Desideria*, for instance, are characteristic of these poems:

> Felices nimium, vitreae, gens caerula, nymphae,
> Membra quibus fluido sunt liquefacta vitro!
> Vosque paludosis mutatae fontibus artus,
> Quae vetus est quondam fama professa mirus.
> Cur mihi non liquidis stillant quoque brachia rivis,
> Glaucaque; muscosis fluctuat unda comis?[10]

Again, there were certain concepts which words might treat in general and spiritualized terms, but which when taken over into picture must be shown in specific and physical terms; and when these concepts returned into ancillary verse, they brought with them the graphic, physical terms of the design in which they had become embodied. Miss Evans cites as an example of verse written to interpret design, the verse written by William Billying in England between 1400 and 1430 to illustrate designs of the Five Wounds of Christ, suitable for glass, painting, or embroidery. The fourth Wound is designed as a wounded hand, rayed, with a scroll inscribed, "i h c the well of grace." The verse runs:

> Hayle welle of grace most precyouse in honoure
> In the Kynges left hande set of ierusalem
> Swetter thanne bawme is thy sweet lycore. . . .[11]

As the emblem fashion developed from its original sources into far more complicated forms, the verse drew upon the picture to intensify its style. For since poetry imitates the experiences of all the senses, it was possible to have emblems, as well as other descriptions, in words. And thus the emblem restored to poetry under a very greatly changed form the allegorical or symbolistic

[10] Hermannus Hugo, *Pia Desideria Emblematis, Elegiis, & Affectibus Illustrata*, (Antverpiae, M.DC. XXVIII.) p. 67.
[11] *Op. cit.*, p. 152.

impulse it had derived from poetry. As the verses from Billying illustrate the relationship in a very simple form, so the style of Quarles' *Emblems* shows this development at its more complex stage. In his Invocation, the figures tumble out so fast that our imaginations hardly have scope to realize them as figures. Thus,

> Cast off these dangling Plummets that so clog
> Thy lab'ring heart, which gropes in this dark fog
> Of dungeon earth, let flesh and blood forbeare
> To stop thy flight.
>
> ..................................................
>
> Let heavens fire season
> The fresh conceits of thy corrected Reason

And among the excessively sensuous figures which load his work, such as,

> Blustering Boreas blows the boyling Tide
> The white-mouthed water now usurps the Shore,

he mixes images which we can feel only emblematically, and not in direct sensuous terms, such as "Th' Icarian wings of babbling Fame," and again mingles literal terms and ingenious figures, as in

> What's here to be enjoy'd
> But griefe, and sicknesse, and large bills of sorrow,
> Drawn now, and crost to-morrow?

This transfer of the emblem into the actual texture of the verse can be strongly felt in the poetry of Crashaw. We have already noted in the *Sospetto* the combination of ingenuity with an ardent symbolization or picturization of idea, a combination not found in his original and giving much of its essential tone to his poem. This combination is thoroughly in the emblematic mode. Take simply the first two examples which offer themselves, in the first two stanzas,

> *O be a Dore*
> *Of language to my infant Lips,* yee best
> Of Confessours: whose Throates *answering his swords,*
> Gave forth your Blood for breath, *spoke soules for words.*

> Great *Anthony*! . . . . . .
> The Beauties of whose dawne *what eye may bide,*
> Which with the Sun himselfe *weigh's equall wings.*

The kinship between the emblem and these images, with their ideational quality, and their newness, "originality," enigmatic tone, is manifest.

Then too, Crashaw's *Sancta Maria Dolorum*, as we have seen, owes the ingenious rhetoric of its passions and much of the rhetorical form of its figures to Marino's *Stabat Mater;* but it is none-the-less different from Marino's *Stabat Mater* both in its feeling and in its essential poetic method. It owes the amplitude of feeling to the original hymn itself as that hymn evokes the whole of the poet's spiritual development. Its figurative method, whereby Crashaw strives to realize the idea as sensuous-emotional perception, is emblematic.

> Eja, Mater, fons amoris,
> Me sentire vim doloris
> Fac ut tecum lugeam.
> Fac ut ardeat cor meum
> In amando Christum Deum,
> Ut sibi complaceam.
>
> O Mother turtle-doue!
> Soft sourse of loue
> That these dry lidds might borrow
> Somthing from thy full Seas of Sorrow!
> O in that brest
> Of thine (the noblest nest
> Both of loue's fires & flouds) might I recline
> This hard, cold, Heart of mine!

Another aspect we have noted in these images of Crashaw is their quaint blending of literal and figurative, of minute detail of resemblance with larger suggestive elements. In so far as this grotesque combination of elements arises merely from the poet's pursuit of physical resemblances, it may owe something to Marinism and to the rhetorics. But it is really very different from the modes established by these books. As we saw in considering the *Sospetto,* it is one of the aspects of his symbolism. Now such effects are, almost inevitably, common in emblematic art. For, first, the aim of this art is to express the ideational that is existent or immanent in the world as the world is literally reported by the senses; and, secondly, as pictorial art, the emblem comes from a long tradition of sensuous directness, and, especially in the case of Dutch and German work, of realism. Following the impulse of this pictorial tradition, in most cases the actual emblem occupies only the foreground of the plate, and stands against a charming landscape or architectural background which is related to the emblem not as an idea, but only as a local habitation, and that often by the slightest thread. In this the art reveals its derivation from tapestry. The emblems of Alciatus, says Miss Evans, show the mediaeval tradition of decorative personifications and garden backgrounds simplified and revised for Renaissance use. The background, for instance, to the allegorical figure of Alciatus' *Sapientia humana,* already alluded to, is a beautifully etched city by the sea; that to Sambucus' fable of *In copia minor error,* a walled city. In his *Vera Amicitia,* the emblem, a large hand emerging from the clouds and holding out a flaming heart to two men in Roman garb with clasped hands, stands against a distant semi-classical landscape. Then, further, while the whole purpose of an emblem itself is focused on its figurative meaning, in many cases what actually delights the reader is the realistic charm of its minute detail. Such an emblem is the *Vae qui praedaris, nonne & ipse praedaberis?* of Daniel Cramer.[12] The emblem represents a woman with a padlock through her lips standing before an anvil with hammer poised and about to strike a heart which she holds on the anvil. The anvil is drawn very realistically, with all the smith's tools lying about it. The whole scene is laid in a mediaeval piazza, with landscape suggested in the background. In this mingling of elements we find again the type of Crashaw's poetry. The startling juxtaposition of highly symbolic design and homely realism of execution is, in technique and imaginative effect, very like Crashaw's

> In this sad House of slow Destruction,
> (His shop of flames) hee fryes himselfe, . . . .

A further quality of Crashaw's style which was apparent in comparing his *Sospetto* with Marino's poem was the existence in him side by side of two opposing tendencies, on the one hand the tendency to abstract imagery from its sensuous context and connotation, on the other the tendency to use a rich sensuous embroidery for background. As we have said, these floriate passages,

---

[12] Daniel Cramer, *Emblemata Moralia nova, Das ist: Achzig Sennreiche Nachdenkliche Figuren auss heyliger Schrifft in Kupfferstücken fürgestellt.* . . . Franckfurt am Mayn. Anno. M. D.C. XXX.

in their whole temper, seem to show the influence of Spenser. And we need hardly remind ourselves that the blending of sensuous richness with spiritual meaning is the warp and woof of Spenser. What is strikingly different in Crashaw from anything in Spenser is the existence side by side in him of the two opposing modes of realization in the imagery itself, the main mode the symbolic one, with the mode of direct sensuous realization serving as decorative background. But these two modes coexist in the emblem proper and in its landscape background. Here again the emblematic in Crashaw's poetry is apparent. Perhaps, also, Crashaw in common with other poets owes something of his floriate richness, directly as well as indirectly, to the beautiful allegorical tapestries with verse which were among the great arts of the Middle Ages and the Renaissance. He was particularly fitted by his temper and interest to feel their influence in so far as he had opportunity to see them, by the high church and Catholic influences with which he was surrounded—one remembers here again the Little Gidding use of continental engravings to illustrate their Concordances—and by the religious themes and the symbolic manner of his poetry. There were such tapestries as the verdure tapestry illustrated by Miss Evans, one of a series of angels bearing the instruments of the Passion. An angel half kneels bearing a pillar and a scourge, beside a great scroll inscribed with a verse in honor of the Passion. Over the angel's head and in the border are crosses; the background is made up of exquisite flowers in fine detail, and among their leaves stand a dog and a fox [?]. The border repeats the flower patterns, with the addition of many birds flying among them.[13] The verse suggests the opening theme of Crashaw's *On the bleeding Wounds of our crucified Lord*, though of course there are other much nearer sources and analogues for that poem. Another tapestry, from the allegorical group, represents *Nature* (a grande dame in elaborate and realistic garb) sending her tufter *Jeunesse* into cover, a verse below this explaining the allegory. The cover, which forms the background, is an elaborate representation of flowers with bushes and trees which in the farthest background at the top and left almost form a landscape in perspective.[14] Certainly one cannot trace a specific influence of these tapestries upon Crashaw, but one ought to have

[13] *Pattern*, plate 202.
[14] *Ibid.*, plate 203.

them in mind as part of the rich context of his background. However, Crashaw's main imagery is closer to the emblematic than to such symbol and allegory as that in the tapestries.

Often, Crashaw's images may be called *imprese* or heroic symbols rather than emblems. The *impresa* or heroic symbol was more concentrated and more abstract even than the emblem; it told no story but summed up a character or a life as the illustration of one ethical or pathetic idea, represented by a single sign. It made no direct sensuous representation of its character or life, or idea (except in so far as the charm of the *impresa,* as pure design, might be felt to have some aesthetic congruity with the idea it figured) but was as purely an abstract symbol as an image can be. Even more perhaps than the emblem, accordingly, *imprese* and heroic symbols were esoteric. Messer Lodovico Domenichi thus sums up the qualities of the *impresa* in his introduction to Bishop Paulo Giovio's *Dialogo Dell' Imprese Militari et Amorose*:[15]

1. It must have just proportion of body and spirit (*D'anima & di corpo*: figure and epigraph).
2. It must be not obscure . . , neither so clear that every common spirit (*plebeo*) can understand it.
3. Above all, it must have sensuous charm (*bella vista*) , . . . stars, suns, moons, flame, water, trees in leaf, mechanical tools, strange animals, & fantastic birds.
4. It must contain no human form.
5. The motto should be commonly in a language different from that of him for whom the *impresa* is made so that the sentiment may be somewhat covered; and it should be brief, yet not so much so as to be either ambiguous or unclear.

If we transfer the first four of these conditions from graphic to linguistic figures, we seem to be describing many of Crashaw's images, such as,

From whence Heav'n-labouring Bees with busie wing,
    Suck hidden sweets, which well digested proves
    Immortall Hony for the Hive of Loves.

Hee saw the Nest
Of pois'nous and unnaturall loves, Earth-nurst;
Toucht with the world's true antidote to burst.

[15] *Dialogo Dell 'Imprese Militari et Amorose.* Di Monsignor Giovio Vescovo di Nocera. Con vn Ragionamento di Messer Lodouico Domenichi, nel medesimo soggetto. (In Lione: 1550.)

Heauens thy fair eyes be;
Heauens of euer-falling starres.
'Tis seed-time still with thee
And starres thou sow'st, whose haruest dares
Promise the earth to countershine
Whateuer makes heaun's forhead fine.

At these thy weeping gates,
(Watching their watry motion)
Each winged moment waits,
Takes his TEAR, & gets him gone.

This last compares interestingly with such an *impresa* as that of Catherine de Medici after the death of Henry II: "broken fans and necklaces and flames drowned in tears, with *Ardorem extincta testantur vivere flamma.*[15a] Or to compare two specific images, consider this from the *De Symbolis Heroicis Libri IX* of the Jesuit Silvestro Petrasancta: The rays of the sun streaming through the clouds upon a heap of eggs, one of which rises towards heaven; the motto: *Quia Rore Plenum.* And the text: *Ovum exemptis vitello ac albumine, ac refertum rore, sursum à Sole trahitur; alia oua, quibus ponderi sunt cognata viscera, humi relinquuntur. Sola post obitum VIRGO DEIPARA in caelum assumitur: quia* gratia plena *prae alias sola fuit,*[16] and then this of Crashaw's *Vexilla Regis,*

Euen ballance of both worlds! our world of sin,
And that of grace heaun way'd in HIM,
Vs with our price though weighed'st;
Our price for vs thou payed'st;
Soon as the right-hand scale reioyc't to proue
How much Death weigh'd more light than loue.

We must not leave the book without noting, finally, with Domenichi, that the *impresa* might easily be and often was absurd, but that the best have "del magnanimo, del genoroso, e dell' acuto, e (come si dice) del frizzante."

The spirit of the *impresa* is present, too, in Crashaw's symbolization of concrete sense adjectives as well as in his images. "Soft" becomes in Crashaw's poetry a pure adjective of sentiment and "white" passes through a sense of radiance or brilliance—perhaps with some recollection of "candidus"— to become a pure

[15a] Described in Joan Evans, *Pattern*, p. 118, n. 2.
[16] *De Symbolis Heroicis*, (Antverpiae: M.DC. XXXIV).

symbol of "exaltation." Here the moral and intellectual impulse is tied up with Crashaw's special quality as an individual,—with that intensity with which he flings himself upon sentiment. On this side it is related to the notable abundance in his poetry of luscious abstract adjectives of sentiment, "gratious," "sullen Cypresse," "sweetly-killing dart," "glorious," "delicious." And yet in general nature the impulse to such sentimental abstraction has much in common with the *impresa.*

And so, taking all the forms we have just illustrated, we may think of the *impresa* and the *impresa*-like image as another special and ingenious mode of expression into which Crashaw forced his art and which, despite its essential imaginative limitations, was made to give scope for Crashaw's ampler utterance once his imagination had transformed it.

As Crashaw develops, his imagery, or as perhaps one ought now to say, his symbolism becomes almost schematic, almost a private scholasticism. Repetition of imagery must be found in any poet writing in this field and trying to describe the ineffable in some ideal form, on any level, as we see, for instance, in Vaughan's images of darkness and light or Shelley's of moonlight and light on moving water. In Crashaw not only images of such scope as *flame* and *sacrifice* but those of more limited connotation like *nest* and *blushes* become elements in a supersensuous scheme. This repetition derives in him both specifically from the emblem and *impresa* and generally from that system of thought which sees this world as one vast alphabet of the other, a system of thought central elements in which are the symbolism of the Mass and the traditional interpretation of the *Song of Songs.* This mode of imagery, much as it has in common with Marino and with the rhetorics in its pure form, has related itself definitely to a universe of coherent meaning in which Marino and the rhetorics do not participate.

So far we have considered chiefly the types and modes of Crashaw's imagery. But as we examine the development of his rhetoric, what it took from its sources, and what it rejected, how it transformed these elements and integrated them, we find the shaping spirit to lie in the energy of the meaning that fills the imagery. Imagery is of supreme significance with Crashaw; in a very special sense his imagery is his meaning. *Le style, c'est l'homme.* With Crashaw, his style is not merely the expression of his taste in the profoundest sense of that word. The seeds of sensation; emotion unfolding from it and like a rising chlorofil drawing energies of thought into its growth; the blossom of symbolic awareness,—this is the ecstatic process of Crashaw's thought. And it is this process of thought that conditions and ultimately transmutes his imagery. Infinitely rich in artifice as is Crashaw's expression there is, in his mature style, almost no pure description, no element of *virtu.* Even in such a *tour de force* as *Musicks Duell,* all the tricks of style and blendings of the different senses somehow integrate to suggest the ecstasy of musical experience. If Crashaw constantly holds up the forward movement of his theme to enrich some centrifugal detail—in contrast to Donne whose thought is analysed through his figure with the drive of a high-voltage current,—it is because in him it is the details of sensation, rising like varied fumes, that constitute perception. Dante Gabriel Rossetti is another illuminating example of the poet whose images are the essential key to his inner life. Rosetti is highly decorative. But among the elaborate and pictorial figures that decorate his themes are others, recurring images, which are symbolic. And it is these symbolic images particularly which illuminate his obscure sonnets as a whole. Thus the image of "the grove," in which single figure Rossetti expresses the love life that he and his beloved share and that separates them from the world, gives us the key to that shadowed thought-world, organized along the lines of force of passion, which conditioned Rossetti's experiencing of the outward facts and relationships of life. This thought world is implicit in, and central to all his sonnets, but never explicitly defined in them; the symbol of "the grove" is the essential definition. And so it is with Crashaw; the symbol is the essential reflection. Hence it arises that where Wordsworth, a poet likewise seeking to integrate his perceptions into certain fundamental concepts, frequently repeats ideas, Crashaw constantly repeats images.

Crashaw's imagery is very distinctive. Yet there is no one element in it not abundantly paralleled in contemporary verse. His sensuousness; his ingenious turn of figure upon the pivot of external physical dimensions; his curious blending of figurative and literal meanings, of emotional and factual—one might almost say of aesthetic and domestic—connotations; even the use of particular characteristic images—"toy," for instance, as a symbol of the worldly or material;—his use of traditional image side by side with the unaccustomed one which yields the ironic gleam of the *species aeternitatis* breaking upon this world, a flash always so fresh and so "metaphysical"; to turn through a dozen pages of any collection of the day is to feel them all. The true distinction of Crashaw's imagery, both in its abundance and in the mode of its use, lies in the attitude toward life it expresses and the way this attitude shapes and transmutes the forms into new molds.

Signor Praz, in speaking of *The Weeper*, compares Crashaw to Shelley and Swinburne in the profusion of images, in the agglomeration of conceits and figures which tend to isolate themselves, lacking a central point around which the poem gravitates in a harmony of parts. But in general there is a fundamental distinction between the profusion of Crashaw and Shelley on the one hand and of Swinburne on the other,—a distinction which helps to define Crashaw. As Shelley and Crashaw mature through sensationalism into aspiration and ecstasy, the wayward abundance of image that leads on image—a thing in its origin far more intellectual and ingenious in Crashaw than in Shelley—yields steadily to a process that concentrates and focuses sense impressions upon some single dominant and symbolic aesthetic consciousness. Swinburne's images, on the contrary, often remain an unhealthy process of proliferation, frequently torturing the image in order to twist the idea to a conclusion beyond the range of the poet's sincere experience either in thought or in emotion. Compare, for instance, the passage on music from Crashaw's hymn *To the One Name*, (quoted at length on page 41) with a passage on the sea from Swinburne's *Triumph of Time*:

> The low down leans to the sea; the stream,
> One loose thin pulseless tremulous vein,
> Rapid and vivid and dumb as a dream,
> Works downward, sick of the sun and the rain;
> No wind is rough with the rank rare flowers;
> The sweet sea, mother of loves and hours,
> Shudders and shines as the grey winds gleam,
> Turning her smile to a fugitive pain.
>
> Mother of loves that are swift to fade,
> Mother of mutable winds and hours,
> A barren mother, a mother-maid,

Cold and clean as her faint salt flowers.
I would we twain were even as she,
Lost in the night and the light of the sea,
Where faint sounds falter and wan beams wade,
Break, and are broken, and shed in showers.

In each the theme is symbolic; in each, the poet unfolds his idea through a pivot upon his image; each gains much of its effect through its musical form and especially through alliteration. But Swinburne gives a series of sensations that, though poignant, are really unrelated, and his purported analysis of idea through the images is in essence really only a verbal manipulation of concepts, so that the Greek concept of the sea as fruitless (unvintaged, ατρύγετος) is pushed to an absurd and grotesque meaninglessness when she becomes a barren mother. Crashaw gives a dominant emotion, and in the end realizes a single concept, through a series of figurative themes and melodic phrases that are all harmonized and subdued to that one emotion & concept. And his design, in its own kind, has architectonic quality, bringing all the elements of sensation within one sweep of line.

Crashaw is, as we have seen, the product of schools and modes of rhetoric as external and as merely dialectic as anything can well be in poetry. Yet his growth through these modes from formality into form and expressiveness is steady and organic. It is interesting to trace several of his images through various periods and see their growth in scope and poetic intensity. Two images used from his earliest poems on through to his latest are that stock Elizabethan character, the *phoenix*, and a *blush*.

A. The Phoenix.

1. Nay. stopp thy [his own Muse's] clowdy eyes. It is not good,
   To droune thy selfe in this pure pearly flood.
   But since they are for fire workes, rather proue
   A Phaenix & in chastest flames of loue
   Offer thy selfe a Virgin sacrifice
   To quench the rage of hellish deities.
   *Upon the gunpowder treason*. Before 1630. (p. 388).

2. Doe I not see a constellation, [the royal family] . . .
   Who would not be a Phaenix, & aspire
   To sacrifice himself in such sweet fire?
   *Upon the Kings coronation*. Before 1630. (p. 389).

3. Such was the brightnesse of this Northerne starre,
It made the Virgin Phœnix come from farre
To be repaird: hither she did resort,
Thinking her father had remou'd his court.
*Upon the Kings Coronation.* Before 1630. (p. 390).

4. In thy faithfull wombe,
That Nest of *Heroes*, all our hopes finde roome.
Thou art the Mother *Phœnix*, and thy Breast
Chast as that Virgin honour of the East,
But much more fruitfull is; nor does, as shee,
Deny to mighty Love a Deity.
Then let the Easterne world bragge and be proud
Of one coy *Phœnix*; while we have a brood
A brood of *Phœnixes*; while we have Brother
And Sister *Phœnixes*, and still the Mother;
And may we long; long mayst thou live t'encrease
The house and family of *Phœnixes*.
Nor may the light that gives their Eye-lids light,
E're prove the dismall Morning of thy Night:
*Vpon the Duke of* Yorke *his Birth*
*A Panegyricke.* 1630-1631. (p. 180).

5. The Sunne . . . .
vow'd to bring
His owne delicious Phœnix from the blest
*Arabia*, there to build her Virgin nest,
To hatch her selfe in,
*Vpon the Death of Mr. Herrys.* 1631. (p. 167).

6. That in the Center of his Brest
(Sweet as is the Phænix nest)
*His Epitaph.* 1631. (p. 173).

7. Let Nature die, if (*Phœnix*-like) from death
Revived Nature take a second breath;
If on *Times* right hand, sit faire *Historie;*
*On the Frontispiece of* Isaacons
*Chronologie explained.* 1633. (p. 191).

8. *Zephirus* . . .
will throw
A fragrant Breath suckt from the spicy nest
O'th pretious Phœnix, warme upon her Breast.
*On a foule Morning being then to*
*take a journey.* By 1635. (p. 182).

9. (Uncertain) This bird [the maydenhead] indeed the phænix was
late chaced by loues revengefull arrowes,

. . . . . . . . . .

She of Cupids shafts afraid
left her owne balme-breathing East
And in a westerne bosome made
a softer and a sweeter neast;

. . . . . . . . . .

And now poore Loue was at a stand

. . . . . . . . . .

At length a fort he did devise
Built in the noble Brampstons eyes
And ayming thence this matchlesse maydenhead
was soon found dead

Yet Loue in death did wayte upon her,
granting leaue she should expire
in her fumes and haue the honour
t' exhale in flames of his own fire;
her funerall pyle
the marriage bedd,
in a sighed smile
she vanished.
So rich a dresse of death nere famed
the Cradles where her kindred flamed;
so sweet her mother phaenixes of th' East
nere spiced their neast:
*Epithalamium* 1635 (?) (p. 406).

10. *Thyr.* Proud world, said I; cease your contest
And let the MIGHTY BABE alone.
The Phænix builds the Phænix' nest.
Love's architecture is his own.
The BABE whose birth embraves this morn,
Made his own bed e're he was born.
*In the Holy Nativity.* (Second version) 1645-1648. (p. 249).

The first instances of the image are ingenious, literally physical, vague in connotation, inorganic to the theme. Following these come instances which connote specific sentiment. The last instances are pure symbol, clarified, with the physical diagram again present, but absorbed into and expanding the connotations of the symbol. The phoenix in the first three instances (all school-boy exercises) is thrust violently into the texture as a fashionable bit of Tyrian. In the fourth it is brought in as a token (far-fetched, indeed) of supreme quality, specifically related to the poet's theme by the highly ingenious reference to the Queen's purity, the phoenix being a pattern of chastity. In the fifth, it figures in a list of supreme excellencies represented as gathered about Herrys; in this instance it is close in meaning to the first three, but it expresses a more definite sentiment than they do. In the sixth, it is purely the sentiment of the figure that counts. In the seventh and in the ninth, though in the latter instance there is much more of mere ingenuity than in the seventh and a fragility suited to the tone of the poem, Crashaw expresses an idea abstracted from the figure, but wrapt in the emotional aura of its sensuous origin. The eighth instance, not improbably very early, reverts to the first three. The tenth is symbol at its purest and richest, concentrated and clarified beyond seven and nine by the now mature integration of the imagination of its maker.

**B. Blushes.**

1. But stay, what glimpse was that? why blusht the day?
   *Vpon the Duke of Yorke his Birth.* 1630-1631. (p. 179).
   (See also 9.)

2. The timourous Maiden-Blossomes on each Bough,
   Peept forth from their first blushes: so that now
   A Thousand ruddy hopes smil'd in each Bud,
   *Vpon the Death of Mr.* Herrys. 1631. (p. 168).

3. *Apollo. . . .*
   Nor more lovely lift'st thy head,
   Blushing from thine Easterne Bed.
   *Vpon the Death of the most desired Mr.* Herrys. 1631. (p. 169).

4. *Unde rubor vestris, & non sua purpura lymphis?*
   *Quae rosa mirantes tam nova mutat aquas? . . . .*
   *Nympha pudica Deum vidit, &* erubuit.
   Epigram on Joann. 2. By 1634 (p. 38).

5. Drinke fayling there where I a guest did shine
   The Water blush'd, and started into Wine.
   *Out of Grotius his Tragedy of Christes sufferinges.* Date ? (p. 399).

6. Such the Maiden Gemme
   By the wanton Spring put on,
   Peeps from her Parent stemme,
   And blushes on the manly Sun:
   *The Teare.* Before 1635. (p. 84).

7. Each Ruby there,
Or Pearle that dare appeare,
Bee its own blush, bee its owne Teare.
*Wishes.*
*To his (supposed) Mistresse.* Before 1635. (p. 196).

8. Scarce had she blood enough, to make
A guilty sword blush for her sake;

. . . . . . . . . . .

Thy wounds shall blush to such bright scarres,
As keep account of the Lambes warres
*In memory of the Vertuous and Learned Lady Madre de Teresa*
1635-45 (pp. 132, 135).

9. Dy, dy, foul misbegotten Monsters; Dy:
Make haste away, or e'r the world's bright Eye
Blush to a cloud of blood.
*Vpon the Duke of* Yorke *his Birth.* (Additions) 1645-1648 (p. 179).

10. Yet are scarce ripe enough at best to show
The redd, but of the blush to thee they ow.
*Vpon two greene Apricockes.* 1645-1648 (p. 220).

11. Why should the white
Lamb's bosom write
The purple name
Of my sin's shame?
Why should his vnstaind brest make good
My blushes with his own heart-blood?
*Charitas Nimia.* 1645-1648. (p. 282).

12. But had thy pale-fac't purple took
Fire from the burning cheeks of that bright Booke
Thou wouldst on her haue heap't vp all
That could be found SERAPHICALL; . . .
Doe then as equall right requires,
Since His the blushes be, & her's the fires,
Resume and rectify thy rude design;
*The Flaming Heart.* 1645-1648. (p. 325).

13. Hail, most high, most humble one!
Aboue the world; below thy SON
Whose blush the moon beauteously marres
And staines the timerous light of starres.
*O Gloriosa Domina.* 1645-1648. (p. 302).

14. Mercy (my iudge) mercy I cry
With blushing Cheek & bleeding ey,

The conscious colors of my sin
Are red without & pale within.

(Ingemisco tamquam reus;
Culpa rubet vultus meus:
Supplicanti parce, Deus.)
*Dies Irae.* 1645-1648. (p. 301).

15. Each wound of Theirs was Thy [a martyr's] new Morning;
And reinthron'd thee in thy Rosy Nest,
With blush of thine own Blood thy day adorning, . . .
*To the Name Above Every Name.* 1645-1648. (p. 245).

In these figures of the *blush* the same progress is apparent as in the phoenix series. There is in one and three the banal anatomical rhetoric; this is enlarged in two and six into the sentimentality of the pathetic fallacy. In seven, by some indefinable alchemy, fussy sentimental figure has become pure and clarified symbol, sentiment, passion. Part of the alchemy perhaps lies in the condensation of expression, but surely this concentration itself is due to no formal impulse but to the inner fact that the poet now draws upon a deeper level of perception. Even nine, lurid and hysterical as it is, has a pressure of terrified passion that gives insight into Crashaw's feeling about the war. In the second part of the eighth, the blush is almost wholly ideational symbol, yet it is through the physical bridge concealed within the ideational symbolism of *blushes* and of *bright* that the poet effects the compressed meditation on man's passage from the realm of our suffering to the realm of glory, and the sensuous connotation of color in the images helps to achieve the effect. So too in the eleventh and in the last examples. What a complex of concepts and sentiments in the eleventh, diffused through what sensations or echoes of sensation! and then the curious physical conceit, strange filament across which we span the gulf from man's frailty to God's suffering pity.

Where the imagery of any poet is most fully a set exercise, we dare hardly say more than that it is so for us. Who shall declare for its creator what ghosts of sentiment may be kept alive by even the most worn of figures, revisiting the glimpses of the moon and making the poet at least to shake his disposition with those thoughts beyond the reaches of his soul that are the vision of poetry. With Crashaw this is even more than normally true. With him the images, however they begin in mere rhetoric, become the thought; and to study the process by which they are filled and given meaning is to study the growth of his spirit. In Crashaw's study of rhetoric, emblem, *impresa*, a dual process of mind was going on. While the study progressed, he was passing from youth to manhood, and to his vocation as a fellow of Peterhouse; from years of still and untroubled unfolding, into the storm of the Civil War and its compelling, irrevocable decisions; from the delight in his own subtle and pliant wit of a young man "shining like a dove's neck," to the denial of the world and of all that wit would exercise herself upon, of the religious devotee. And as part of his transition, this study of rhetoric and emblem and *impresa* was for Crashaw, as we have already suggested, a kind of intellectual discipline akin in the artistic realm to the discipline, in the religious realm, of mastering the technique of meditation. It was an ordering of sensations and emotions in relation to each other and to a conceptual focus, as apart from mere random fancy or fragmentary ecstasy. At the same time, from the other side, from other and deeper sources of his growth and feeling, the images are transmuted from intellectual forms to imaginative experiences. They have become at once the instrumentalities and the expression of his religious emotion. We have now to study the poetry by and in which Crashaw lives for us, that in which the forms are at last compelled by the poetic vision they give shape to.

## Chapter VI

# STYLE AND SPIRIT FUSED

At twenty-four or twenty-five, Crashaw had mastered the Spenserian manner, with its tender sentiment, its sensuous richness. Nor, though he flashed it only in fragments and did not command it for any large whole, was his manner a mere sympathetic reflection of Spenser. A single line of two from those already quoted is enough to make us feel how preëminently he, among the Spenserians, had been touched with the very spirit of Spenser; this of the Erinnys coming by night to the palace of Herod,

> **And with soft feet searches the silent roomes,**

or this of the mystery of the Incarnation of Christ,

> **And life it selfe weare Deaths fraile Livery.**

He had also, at moments, in some of his details a profound gift of naturalistic interpretation, radiant and intense, which is suggestive of the young Shakespeare, as in that line of the wings,

> **Which like two Bosom'd sailes embrace the dimme Aire.**

And yet, strangely, when he was already master of such powers, he deliberately eschewed and withdrew from these beautiful modes of expression, which were so perfected in their simplicity, so concentrated and so mature; choosing rather to seek his way in a technique that dissolved their achieved unity. He spent himself on technical exercises that, certainly in effect at least,—in their power, that is, of communicating to us—cease to deal with what is central and engage the imagination in surface ingenuities and trivialities.

To many readers of Crashaw it will seem that he turned from Spenser and from direct interpretativeness because he could not face the intellectual and imaginative endeavor necessary to sustain and fill with substance Spenser's manner, and that in him sensuous ecstasy was as it were a short circuit blocking out the ampler vision. And it is true, indeed, that he could have said nothing in the same sort which would have had the scope of Spenser's poetry because, far as he could have gone on in the mature spirit of Spenser, and exquisite as might have been the product, such a development would not have realized Crashaw's own sincere maturity, nor could he have expressed in it more than a fraction of himself. Certain essential qualities he and Spenser had in common; in others they were far apart. In both him and Spenser, there lay behind the manner the pure sensibility which subdues all things to the dream of beauty, the sense that all things exist only as they exist in beauty. But the vision of a positive ethical law, of a chivalric ideal, penetrating and ordering the reason, and thereby transmuting and idealizing man's life, was not Crashaw's vision. Spenser is an individual immersed in the traditional vision of a whole society, and realizing his personal passion through that immersion. Crashaw's is, on the other hand, an intensely self-conscious mind, seeking to realize itself in the very personal integration of that self-consciousness.

Donne, too, had an intensely self-conscious mind, and to think of Crashaw's mind in comparison with his is illuminating. Donne's poetry is filled with that perpetual analysis of his own emotions which constitutes his psychological realism; and his eager and restless intellectual questioning of life in terms of the impinging of his own experience upon the accepted sanctions and concepts forms one of the great springs of his emotion, and is always a large part of its content. Crashaw does not question life as does Donne, and the intellectual analysis of his own emotion is not a large element of his poetry. Indeed such analysis is present in Crashaw only in the accounts which he gives—numerous and important it is true—of his passage into a state of ecstasy. But, despite this unanalytical temper, his was nevertheless a mind highly aware of its own intellections; conscious, that is, of the process of its religious exercises, of its own motions toward meditation and toward self-examination, of the process of its own concentration and unification. For in minds of any degree of sophistication there may be going on constant processes of intellection which on the one hand, may grow from the deep levels of thought among those concepts that are not merely verbal but that are experiential realities—the result of intense observation—; or they may be, as we have said in considering the function of symbolic language, verbal intellections, on the surface of the mind. And, again, once articulated they may rest in the mind as intellections or they may feed back into the larger movements of the mind, into that organic blend of awareness, of emotion, of long formed reflections and of new reasonings,—which is the ultimate thought of a man or of a poet. It was this process of integrating all intellection with the fuller movements of thought that Crashaw worked so intensely and so consciously to achieve. His mind was early filled with ardor. This ardor he wished to relate by a system of analysis to a context of ampler meaning. To this end he engaged deliberately in exercises which begin in mere verbal and rhetorical formalism; but, as we have seen, he used the forms as premises, as starting points, for reflection on something much ampler; reflection on that relation between the two worlds of matter and of idea which his emotions were already engaged in trying to understand. And he was self-conscious of this mode of reflection, and of his own progress in it. If he would realize his experience to the full, he must fuse the exercises with the ardor.

As we saw in studying his life, he must have been from a very early stage a person of intense sensibility, prone to ecstasy. As vivid capacity for sensation grew in him into larger emotion, he sought to abstract from particular emotions a state of pure emotion. Then side by side with this sensationalism, on which his imagination and his powers of expression were most immediately at work, there came a course of reflections. This series of reflections comprehended, first, the meditations which give body to the Latin epigrams. Then, second, in the images based on Marino and the textbooks and handbooks of rhetoric, Crashaw constructed a series of rhetorical syllogisms, and this construction of syllogisms was a process of thought which indeed always remained verbal and trivial in its technique, but which was an intellectual exercise, too, and was used by Crashaw to create in substance a schematic and dialectic account of that symbolism wherewith this material world symbolizes spiritual reality. Third, in emblem and *impresa*, he prosecuted a more intensive study of symbolism and a more intensive reflection on the ideas symbolized in his own work. As he wrote and reflected in terms of epigrammatic paradoxes, of ingenious metaphors, of emblems, these forms must have modified the very nature of his sensations, loading with connotations every simple experience and thus changing the content of the emotions that sprang from each. But even in the subtle web of these complexes the original pure intensity of his sensations and their ecstatic energy did not fade; it was indeed from their energy that the dry dialectic of the reflective exercises drew sap and vigor. This changed and interwoven character of sensation and of reflective expression, Crashaw sought to impress, as we have seen, upon the very nature of his language; for he must break violently through the old modes to an expression that carried with it the summation of his own experience. Thus, to body forth his cumulated experience, he had created as the form of his literary expression that symbolism it has been our task to study. This form was not like those great traditional formulations of human thought and experience to which many of the writers of the seventeenth century owed so much, and which at moments seem to give the perception of the ages as a gift to poets not in themselves profoundly gifted in insight. It was a formulation dependent on many personal and momentary elements of experience. Since it was so, it needed the full growth of Crashaw's personality to change a mere ingenious technique into an organic style.

Even in the most artificial poems that personality was never wholly absent. Even in the early work of the Ovidian epigrams, amid the stylized Ovidian rhetoric, there were elements of serious moral and religious reflection, distinctive of Richard Crashaw and rather massive in their total effect. And though in the first Marinism of *The Weeper*, of the English epigrams, and of the fugitive translations from the classics, this concern with high thought seemed to give way to trivial ingenuity, and, at best, to a certain mere lyricism of the sensations, yet the deeper interests of Crashaw's nature were always reaching toward meditation; and in the *Sospetto*, the sensuousness and the ingenuity are surcharged with the impulse to integrate themselves with larger meanings and with sublimated emotions. The literary activity on religious themes was itself one of the important forces in the growth of Crashaw's mind. Meanwhile, far more of his energy than he put into his writing went to serious reading and to the life of meditation and prayer. At first in this life sensuous ecstasy was the most fully realized note. As his personal religion matured, however, certain traditional meditative themes lie side by side in Crashaw's imagination with his ecstatic experiences. I do not know whether one may speak of the content of ecstasy. And ecstasy, and not philosophical reflection, "the concentration of reason in feeling" which Jowett defined as Platonic mysticism, is the experience which Crashaw voices in his poetry. But in the last and greatest poems, the connotations of the grand meditative themes of Catholic religion are bound in with the sensations, the figures, the symbols, that express the ecstasy. The crushing of the personal and bodily man to humility and spiritual desire through participation in the Passion; the abyss which divides the grayness of man's ordinary state from the state of ecstasy, aesthetic or religious; man's tragic and fading life,—no theme or figure is voiced more often or with more certain pathos than that of man as the dark son of dust and sorrow; the glory of God's gift of himself to man;—these are the themes of the hymns.

Some of the mature poems illustrate the whole process of Crashaw's development at work. *The Office of the Holy Crosse* and the versions of the mediaeval hymns are such poems. They are the least satisfying of Crashaw's mature work. In them more than in his other late work we are teased by the trivial and the ingenious. If we look at them purely objectively, and without relation to Crashaw's inner history, we might be tempted to say that they carry forward the worst mechanicalness of his early work, and that their over-elaboration, which loses the design of the whole in detail, is in the very nature of the baroque; that the complex oversubtleties of idea and image are in the very nature of a system of thought that has passed its prime and become too sophisticated, with the result that the techniques of intellection are too readily handled tools, and tempt the poet to rest in his skilled play with them, and not in any substantial design made by them. But the cause lies far deeper. To secure a form for a new and personal energy of poetry Crashaw had apprenticed his art and his forms of thought to techniques so rigid and artificial and in themselves so barren that it required all the intensity of his ecstasy and all the sweep of his passion to instill in them inner imaginative life. And in these hymns, Crashaw was in part prevented from instilling such life because he was not handling his material freely. He wrote them stanza by stanza, bound to their originals without surrendering himself to the spirit of them. In the result, the old vision which gave unity and concentration to his great originals is broken up, and yet he has not room or freedom for a new integration of his own. The originals are objective and concentrate upon the definition of the religious idea or figure or story or obligation which is their theme. Crashaw is subjective, as we have seen he always was, and he seeks to express his own consciousness of his participation in the experience that is his theme, and his self-examination as to his progress in the realization of it. *Sancta Maria Dolorum*, the translation of the *Stabat Mater*, may serve our study as a type of them all. In it Crashaw is in difficulty from the outset in trying to realize two very distinct conceptions, on the one hand that of the original, with its self-forgetful absorption in the great type of human suffering, and in the poet's desire to surrender the self to the larger meaning of that pain; and on the other the conception of Marino with his rhetorical passions, his vulgar dramatization, his brilliant wit. As a result of this divided conception, and of the segmental development stanza by stanza already aluded to, Crashaw's own poetic vision fails to absorb wholly his poetic method. The wit in the metaphors overweighs the element of larger meditation, and many of them have not that concentration to achieve which Crashaw needed the full sweep of his passion. Thus, we have the grotesqueness of,

> Shall I, sett there
> So deep a share
> (Dear wounds) & onely now
> In sorrows draw no Diuidend with you?

But yet there is in the poem a real anguish of self-destruction, kindled in part by the original, and in part by the whole course of Crashaw's religious reading and exercise:

> That these dry lidds might borrow
> Somthing from thy full Seas of sorrow!
> O in that brest
> Of thine . . . . . .
> might I recline
> This hard, cold, Heart of mine!

In this divided purpose and imperfect diffusion of ardor through the images of intricate wit, the genetic history of his evolution in style and consciousness is present.

So in the mediaeval hymns as a whole. All the literary modes that Crashaw practised are present in them, all striving toward an integrating passion which, however, they achieve only in moments. Side by side are the Marinistic or rhetorical devices which splinter thought and dissolve emotion and the curious dialect of emblematism, deepened by the meditative mode of the early epigrams. And since Crashaw's first effort in meditation, the paradox and the intellectual analysis themselves have gained in intensity and profundity, though not in clarity. Then, shot through these ingenious processes of thought and through the deepening tones of meditation, is the pure poet's recreative vision, the emotion that would calcine them to unity, sublimating sensation and inspiriting ingenuity till they blend in symbol. The finest poetry in the translations of the Latin hymns is found in the symbolic epigrams which abound in them.

> The world's price sett to sale, & by the bold
> Merchants of Death & sin, is bought and sold.
>
> And from the nailes & spear
> Turn'd the steel point of fear,
> Their vse is chang'd, not lost; and now they moue
> Not stings of wrath, but wounds of loue.
>
> Call if you can
> Harpes of heaun to hands of man.
>
> . . . . . . . . . .
>
> When LIFE, himself, at point to dy
> Of loue, was his own LEGACY.

Though Crashaw never realized his feeling fully in the mediaeval hymns, the passion at work within them flashes forth in a moment in these epigrams. But in general, the imagery in them is discordant and still technical. So too the music. They have no musical design as units; only fragments of music, of which the greatest are the chord-like effects of the epigrams. Of them all, the finest, though the least grand in theme, is *O Gloriosa Domina*. It is the finest largely because in it Crashaw most freely leaves his original and develops his own feeling as a unit without being bound to the original stanza by stanza. The original theme of this hymn, too, lends itself best of any of them to Crashaw's typical ecstasy. The resulting poem has the most of his peculiar radiance.

Of Crashaw's original hymns, the most tender both in its theme and in its treatment is the hymn of the shepherds, *In the Holy Nativity*. As we have seen, it was written before the others, probably as early as 1642, and it mingles with the elements of physical minutiae which came from Italian influences much that is close to the pellucid Spenserian sensuousness and sentiment,

> We saw thee in thy baulmy nest,
> Bright dawn of our aeternall Day!
> . . . . . . . . . . .
> Yet when young April's husband showrs
> Shall blesse the fruitfull Maja's bed
> We'l bring the First-born of her flowrs . . .

But mingled with this sensuousness are the metaphysical symbolism and paradox into which Crashaw had at last worked the witty techniques. Now, however, in this final mingling of ardor and dialectic form, the symbols and paradoxes are no longer mere analytical diagrams but spring to life in immediate realization and with Crashaw's never lost sensuous radiance, as in the full chorus, "Welcome, all Wonders in one Sight!" or in the later added phoenix stanza.

The St. Teresa poems, the hymn *In the Epiphanie* and that *On the One Name* have the most grandeur and the most splendor of Crashaw's work. And in the St. Teresa poems, though they have not the sustained musical splendor of the other two, Crashaw most fully realized himself. In the *Hymn, In the Glorious Epiphanie of Our Lord*, great as it is, there are some elements of thought not fully mastered. It is based on the Περι Μυστικης Θεολογιας of Dionysius, and works up in the conclusion to a definition of the negative way which is the subject of the treatise of Dionysius. But, full of rapture though the poem is, I do not think this concept of the negative way in all its scope has been fully realized by Crashaw, or fully absorbed into the growth of Crashaw's own mind; and the statement of the concept does not flower from the vision of the poem as a whole, but seems added to it. The true original concept of the poem, the concept of self-annihilation step by step up through the long process of first realizing, and then sublimating and annihilating, the world, is expressed with Crashaw's utmost fervor. This idea he embodies in the single paradoxical symbol on which the whole poem is built, the symbol of the sun in eclipse at the Passion. The sun, which is the apparent light (of this world) and which has drawn all men's worship to it, casts a dark shadow upon reality. And so when reality is manifested to the world in the true light of Christ, the sun for three hours puts on darkness, in recognition of that reality and in realization of its truer self. And so like the sun must man surrender the world and the intellect to lose himself in vision. To aid us in achieving the vision the poet evokes the pageant of religious history and all rich sensations, as symbols. And even more in this poem than in the mediaeval hymns, Crashaw's new symbolism is a summation of all those evolving elements of his consciousness and of his expression by which he had arrived at the perception here expressed of man's relation to the universe. All those evolving elements are still present in it, in their original forms, though with significances how changed in the new context! Every metaphor of his poetry from the earliest days is repeated in this poem. Then too, not only are the parts expressed in symbols, but as we have seen, the whole is built upon one symbol, and a paradoxical symbol. And the sensuous terms of this symbol act upon us as a continuous excitement that seeks to make us rather "feel than hear" its conceptual meaning. The adjectives and adverbs are a striking force in this strange mingling of the emotional and the analytical, and strikingly illustrate it.

Bright BABE! Whose *awfull* beautyes make
The morn incurr a *sweet* mistake;
For whom the' *officious* heauns deuise
To disinheritt the sun's rise,
*Delicately* to displace
The Day, & plant it fairer in thy face;

All-circling point. All centring sphear.
The world's one round, Æternall year.
Whose full & *all-vnwrinkled* face
Nor sinks nor swells with time or place;
But euery where & euery while
Is One *Consistent solid* smile;
Not vext & tost
'Twixt spring and frost,

Nor by alternate shredds of light
*Sordidly* shifting hands with shades & night.

The *dire* face of inferior DARKNES, kis't
And courted in the *pompous* mask of a *more specious* mist.

Subtle ideas and primary sensations lie side by side in the poem as they have been wrought together in the mind of the poet. And again, like the mediaeval hymns, the poem reaches its climaxes of intensity in the ecstatic and sensuously wrought epigrams.

*The Hymn To the Name above Every Name, The Name of Iesus* has for its theme the enraptured contemplation of the meaning of Christ (Perhaps suggested by the Περι Ονοματων of Dionysius the Areopagite, though there is no theological or philosophical element in Crashaw's treatment). This contemplation of the name Crashaw celebrates by an account of the de-personalizing and elevation of the senses through ecstasy and through intellectual and spiritual vision, taking musical ecstasy as the type or copy of spiritual ecstasy through which the poet transcends to contemplation. It is the senses, organized and enlarged by a great art, which the poet calls upon to lift him from out the dull world of daily perception. It is the concept of Christ which must translate the senses themselves. We are at the heart of Crashaw's vision in such lines as these,

Powres of my Soul, be Proud!
And speake lowd
To all the dear-bought Nations This Redeeming Name,
And in the wealth of one Rich WORD proclaim
New Similes to Nature.
May it be no wrong
Blest Heauns, to you, & your Superiour song,
That we, dark Sons of Dust & Sorrow,
A while Dare borrow
The Name of Your Delights & our Desires,
And fitt it to so farr inferior LYRES.
Our murmurs haue their Musick too,
Ye mighty Orbes, as well as you,
Nor yields the noblest Nest
Of warbling SERAPHIM to the eares of Loue,
A choicer Lesson then the ioyfull BREST
Of a poor panting Turtle-Doue.

That vision proclaims the power of ecstasy,—and this poem contains Crashaw's most intense description of the consciousness as it passes into ecstasy—proclaims the power of an idea, not defined or established, but accepted and felt in all the senses, to catalyse the varied threads and processes of the mind, the varied processes of formulation, the discordant connotations, and reduce them to pure awarenesses of God. These elements Crashaw does not, in our ordinary sense, digest or analyze into thought; he realizes them directly as a state of consciousness.

The hymn is rich in the magic of Elizabethan sensousness. At the same time it abounds in emblems and in the strange intellectualism of Crashaw's symbols, as, to take only one instance, the symbol of the architects of Intellectuall Noise, which is blended with a direct and sensuously abundant description of actual music.

In both this poem and that on the Epiphany, Crashaw called in the power of a simpler emotional fervor to help realize the intellectually more complex one. In both he used figure to define the simpler emotion and the more complex idea as well. In both, some of the images and at the same time the concepts tied up in them still depend too much on an element in their symbolism personal to Crashaw. And this dependence prevents them from being quite immediately apprehensible to us, if we are aware of them and try to realize them separately rather than accepting the poem as a cloud of suggestion. And in both poems some images are not enough energized by the prevailing emotion of the whole poem to have been transmuted from mere ingenuities into expressions of insight, and so in verbal expression, these images are not wholly unified and living. But in both poems, the sensuous emotional ecstasy by which Crashaw approaches the central theme of the poem, failing somewhat in its images, finds another and complete form of expression in the verse music. And in the full tide of feeling along which we are swept by the intoxication of that music, all the elements are absorbed and subdued to one. It is literally through musical ecstasy that Crashaw lifts us into his theme, as it is through the music that he lifts himself into his experience.

The St. Teresa poems, *A Hymn to the Name and Honor of the Admirable Sainte Teresa,* and *The Flaming Heart,* beautiful, magical as their music is, have in the nature of their structure far less musical grandeur than the two poems of which we have just spoken. In compensation, they have a more absolute realization, for us and by Crashaw, of their theme. In the immediate communion with a profounder intellect and spirit than his own, Crashaw fully realized his whole self more than he could in expressing the abstract ideas toward which the other two hymns reach. The imagery is concentrated at all moments, and into something larger than sensuous ecstasy. In these hymns the anguish and the assuaging vision of rapture lie bare before us, in the radiant pictures and in the cry of the epigrams which abound in the poems. Reading the life of Crashaw, we feel the pathos of life closing in upon him at the age of thirty-six; the loneliness and the pain of the last six of those years; the devoted life at Cambridge in ruins about him; the sense of disintegration in the alien world of Leyden; the uncertainty and unrest at Paris; the hint of bitter suffering and of disillusion at Rome. But in the growth of those years, we feel when we read the last words on St. Teresa, he has learned to get behind all techniques and all surface movements of the mind to expression, and behind circumstance and the limitations of ecstasy to his vision:

> **O thou vndaunted daughter of desires!**
> **By all thy dowr of LIGHTS & FIRES;**
> **By all the eagle in thee, all the doue;**
> **By all the liues & deaths of loue;**
> **By thy larg draughts of intellectuall day,**
> **And by thy thirsts of loue more large then they; . . .**
> **Let me so read thy life, that I**
> **Vnto all life of mine may dy.**

# BIBLIOGRAPHY

[This book was substantially finished over two years ago. I have therefore made no attempt to cover all the literature which may have appeared since that time, though I have been able to take account of several items. Of the large body of background material essential to such a study, both in the great body of verse and prose of the period and in critical and scholarly studies, I have listed only those books which bear directly on Crashaw, or from which I have cited, and in the case of editions of poets, only those few volumes not readily accessible to the reader or which, as in the case of Mr. Kastner's edition of Drummond, contain scholarly material bearing directly on this study.]

# PRIMARY SOURCES


ALCIATI, ANDREA. Emblemata. Lyons, 1551.?

ANONYMOUS. The Arminian Nunnery: or a brief description and relation of the late erected monasticall place, called the Arminian Nunnery, at little Gidding in Huntington-Shire. London, 1641.

ANONYMOUS. Bel-vedère or The Garden of Muses. London, 1600.

ANONYMOUS: Wren's Anatomy. Discovring His Notorious pranks, and shameful wickednesse . . . both in his government at Peter-house Colledge . . . London, 1641.

BARCLAY, JOHN. Argenis. Editio novissima. Amsterdam 1664.

BAUHUSIUS, BERNARDUS. Epigrammatum Libri V. Editio altera, auctior. Antwerp, 1620.

BAUHSIUS, BERNARDUS et CABILLAVUS, BALDUINUS. Epigrammata. CAROLUS MALAPERTIUS. Poemata. Antwerp 1634.

BIDERMANUS JACOBUS. Epigrammatum Liber Primus and Heroum Epistolae Epigrammata et Herodias. Bound with the preceding item.

BUCHLERUS,JOANNIS à Gladbach. Thesaurus Phrasium Poeticarum, priore multo accommodatior locupletiorque, cui ad calium adiecta est Institutio Poëtica ex R. P. Iac. Pontani libris desumpta . . . Cologne, 1603.

BUCHLERUS, JOANNIS. Sacrorum Profanarumque Phrasium Poeticarum Thesaurus. Recens Perpolitus & numerosior factus, editio undecima. London, 1632.

CABILLAVUS, BALDUINUS. Epigrammata Selecta. Antwerp, 1620.

CABILLAVUS, BALDUINUS. See BIDERMANUS.

CELLOTIUS, LUDOVICUS. Opera Poetica. Paris, 1630.

COLERIDGE, H. J., S. J. The Life and Letters of Saint Teresa. London 1881

COLLAERT, ADRIAN. [A series of 25 plates illustrative of the life of Saint Teresa]. [Antwerp, 1550?]

CRAMER, DANIEL. Emblemata Moralia Nova, Das ist: Achzig Sinnreiche Nachdenckliche Figuren auss heyliger Schrifft in Kupfferstücken furgestellet. Frankfort a.M., 1630.

CRASHAW, RICHARD. For items on his life and works, see the note on *Poems,* edited by L. C. Martin.

CRASHAW, RICHARD. Carmen Deo Nostro, Te Decet Hymnus, Sacred Poems, edited by J. R. Tutin. London, [1897.]

CRASHAW, RICHARD. The Religious Poems, edited by R. A. Eric Shepard. London, 1914.

CRASHAW, RICHARD. The Poems English Latin and Greek, edited by L. C. Martin. Oxford, 1927.
(This is the definitive edition of Crashaw. It contains a list of the manuscript sources of Crashaw, of the early printed editions and texts—with the exception of the poem in *Iusta Eduardo King*—noted by me—, and an account of the important modern editions. It contains, also, in the Introduction and in Appendix II, the primary data for Crashaw's life, with the exception of one item given by Confrey, one by Nethercot, several important items by Warren, and several items which I have listed under William Crashaw. Accordingly, I have not listed in this bibliography the items already available and brought together in Mr. Martin's work.)

CRASHAW, WILLIAM. Ad Severinum Binnium. Epistola commonitoria super conciliorum generalium editione ab ipso nuper adornata. London, 1624.

CRASHAW, WILLIAM. Complaint or Dialogue Betwixt the Soule & the Bodie of a damned man . . . Supposed to be written by S. Bernard . . . London, 1616.

CRASHAW, WILLIAM. Another edition. London, 1632.

CRASHAW, WILLIAM. Falsificationum Romanarum et Catholicarum restitutionum Tomi Primi liber primus. London, 1606.

CRASHAW, WILLIAM. The Jesuites gospel. London, 1610.

CRASHAW, WILLIAM. The Parable of Poyson in Five Sermons of Spiritual Poyson . . . London, 1618.

CRASHAW, WILLIAM, Manuale catholicorum a manuall for true Catholickes. London, 1611. Sub-title: A Handful or Rather a Heartfull of holy meditations and Prayers. Gathered out of certaine ancient Manuscripts written 300 years ago or more.)

CRASHAW, WILLIAM. Another edition of the same, London, 1631-1632.

CRASHAW, WILLIAM. The Sermon Preached at the Crosse, Feb. xiiij, 1607. London, 1608.

CRASHAW, WILLIAM. A Dialogue Concerning this Question, where was your Church before Luther and Calvin. . . . By W. C. London, 1623. (Printed, with separate title page, in An answer to Mr. Fisher the Jesuite. . . . by Mr. Rogers. London, 1623.)

CRASHAW, WILLIAM A Mittimus to the Jubile at Rome: or, the rates of the Popes Custome-House. Sent to the Pope. . . . And faithfully published out of the old Latin Copie, with Observations upon the Romish text, by William Crashaw. London, 1625.

CRASHAW, WILLIAM. A Sermon preached in London before the right honorable the Lord Lawarre, Lord Governour and Captaine Generall of Virginea . . . Febr. 21, 1609. London, 1610.

CRASHAW, WILLIAM. translator. The New Man. Or, a supplication from an unknowne person, a Roman Catholicke unto Iames, the monarch of Great Britaine, . . . London, 1622. (The translation is stated to be made from the "author's copy," which had come to Crashaw from an English Gentleman who had it from a friend of the author after his death.)

CRASHAW, W., translator. The Italian Convert. Newes from Italy, of a second Moses: or, The Life of Galeocius Caracciolus, . . . Containing the story of his admirable conversion from Popery . . . Written first in Italian, thence translated into Latin by reverend Beza, and for the benefit of our people put into English. London, 1635. (First Edition, 1608.)

CRASHAW, WILLIAM, editor. Consilium delectorum Cardinalium et aliorum Praelatorum de Emendanda Ecclesia . . . 1538 . . . ex Bibliotheca W. Crashaui. London, 1609.

CRASHAW, WILLIAM, editor. Of the calling of the Ministerie. Two treatises, discribing the Duties and Dignities of that Calling. London, 1605. (This contains an Epistle Dedicatory by William Crashaw. W. Perkins is the author.)

CRASHAW, WILLIAM, editor. St. Augustine. Of the Citie of God: with the Learned Comments of Io. Ludovicus Vives. Englished first by I. H. And now in this second Edition compared with the Latine Originall, and in very many places corrected and emended. London, 1620. (Contains a dedicatory epistle to the Earls of Pembroke and Arundel, signed by W. Crashawe, who presumably revised it.)

DIONYSIUS AREOPAGITA. ΠΕΡΙ ΜΥΣΤΙΚΗΣ ΘΕΟΛΟΓΙΑΣ
Migne, Patrologia E. Graecae, Volume 3. Paris, 1889.

DIONYSIUS AREOPAGITA ΠΕΡΙ ΘΕΙΩΝ ΟΝΟΜΑΤΩΝ
Migne, Volume 3. Paris, 1889.

DRUMMOND, WILLIAM OF HAWTHORNDEN. The Poetical Works, with a Cypresse Grove, Edited by L. Kastner. Manchester, 1913.

FERRAR, NICHOLAS. The Actions and Doctrine and other Passages touching our Lord . . . Jesus Christ, as they are related by the Foure Evangelists, reduced into one complete body of Historie. 1635. (One of the Little Gidding Concordances.)

FERRAR, NICHOLAS and his Community. Acta Apostolorum elegantiss. monochromatis delineata. 1635?

FERRAR, NICHOLAS. The Story Books of Little Gidding. Being the Religious Dialogues recited in the Great Room 1631-1632. From the original Manuscript of Nicholas Ferrar. With an Introduction by E. Cruwys Sharland. London, 1899.

GIOVIO, PAULO. BISHOP. Dialogo Dell' Imprese Militari et Amorose. Lyons, 1557.

FONDANUS, M. Phrases Poeticae seu Sylvae Poeticarum Locutionum Uberrimae, Quarum prima vestigia a M. Fundano posita, deinde ab A.S.I.T. auctiores factae. Rouen, 1618.

HUGO, HERMANNUS. Pia desideria emblematis, elegiis, & affectibus illustrata. Antwerp, 1628.

IMPERIALE, GIO. VINCENZO. La Beata Teresa. Genoa, 1615.

LESSIUS, LEONARDUS. Hygiasticon: or, The right course of preserving Life and Health unto extream old Age: . . . The third Edition. Cambridge, 1636.

LL[UELYN], M[ARTIN]. Men-Miracles. With other Poemes. (Oxford?), 1646.

MALAPERTIUS, CAROLUS. Poemata. See BAUHUSIUS, BERNARDUS.

MARINO, GIOVANNI BATTISTA. Adone. Florence, n.d. (Adriano Salani)

MARINO, GIOVANNI BATTISTA. Idilii Favolosi. (In *Collezione Di Classici Italiani* con note) Turin, 1923.

MARINO, GIOVANNI BATTISTA. La Lira. Rime del Cav. Marini. Venice, 1653.

MARINO, GIOVANNI BATTISTA. Poesie Varie, a cura di Benedetto Croce. (n.p.) 1913.

MARINO, GIOVANNI BATTISTA. La Strage De Gl' Innocenti. Venice, 1664.

MAYOR, J. E. B. Edited, Cambridge in the Seventeenth Century. Part I, Nicholas Ferrar. Cambridge, 1855.

OWENI, JOAN. Epigrammatum, Editio Postrema. Amsterdam, 1657.

PETRASANCTA, SILVESTRO. De symbolis heroicis Libri IX. Antwerp, 1634.

PONTANUS, JACOBUS (SPANMULLER.) Institutio Poetica, Ex R. P. Iacobi Pontani . . . Libris Cóncinnata . . . Opera M. Ioannis Buchler à Gladbach, Cologne, 1602. (Published with Buchler's Thesaurus, 1603).

PONTANUS, JACOBUS. Reformata Poeseos Institutio. . . . Editio Novissima Prioribus correctior, auctior pudicior. (n.p., n.d.: in the eleventh edition of Buchler. London, 1632).

PONTANUS, JACOBUS. Progymanasmatum Latinitatis, sive Dialogorum Volumen Primum. Ingolstad, 1594.

QUARLES, FRA:. Divine Fancies: digested into epigrammes, meditations, and observations. London, 1632.

QUARLES, FRA:. Divine Poems, Revised and Corrected with Additions by the Author. London, 1669.

QUARLES, FRA:. Emblemes. London, 1635-34.

REMONDUS, FRANCISCUS. Epigrammata et Elegiae. Antwerp, 1605.

RIBERA, R. P. FRANCISCO, è S. J. Vita B. Matris Teresae De Jesu . . . Cologne, 1620.

SAMBUCUS, JOAN:. Emblemata et Aliquot Nummi antiqui. Quarta editio.

SCALIGER, JULIUS CAESAR, Poetices libri septem, [Lyons] 1561.

SHERBURNE, EDWARD. Salmacis. Lyrian and Sylvia. . . . London, 1651.

T . . . , M . . . The Flaming Hart or the Life of the Glorious S. Teresa. Antwerp, 1642.

TANSILLO, LUIGI. Le Lagrime di San Pietro. Venice, 1738.

TERESA OF AVILA, SAINT. The Life of Saint Teresa, written by herself. Translated from the Spanish by J. Dalton. London, 1851.

TERESA of AVILA, SAINT. The Letters, a complete edition translated from the Spanish and annotated by the Benedictines of Stanbrook, vols. I-IV. London, 1919.—

TERESA OF AVILA, SAINT. Meditations after Communion; or, Exclamations of a Soul to God, translated by the Right Reverend Dr. Milner. Second edition. London, 1812.

TERESA OF AVILA, SAINT. Minor Works, translated from the Spanish by the Benedictines of Stanbrook. London, 1913.

TERESA OF AVILA, SAINT. The Way of Perfection and Conceptions of the Divine Love. Translated from the Spanish by the Reverend John Dalton. London, 1852.

TESAURO, EMMANUELE. Il Cannocchiale Aristotelico. Settima Impressione. Bologna, 1675.

VALDESSO, JOHN. The Divine Considerations. Translated by Nicholas Ferrar with George Herbert's Prefatory Epistle. London, 1905.

VARIOUS. Justa Edouardo King, Naufrago ab Amicis Moerentibus, Amoris & μνείας χαριν Cambridge, 1638.

VARIOUS: Lirici Marinisti. A cura di Benedetto Croce. Bari, 1910.

VOSSIUS, Joannis Gerardus. De Artis Poeticae Natura, ac Constitutione Liber. Amsterdam, 1647.

WHITNEY, JEFFREY. Whitney's "Choice of Emblems." A Facsimile Reprint. Edited by Henry Green. London, Chester, and Nantwich, 1866.

### MANUSCRIPTS

BRITISH MUSEUM: Ms. 12, 497. CAESAR PAPERS.

BRITISH MUSEUM: Ms. Brit. Bibl. Cotton. Julius Caesar III.

## SECONDARY SOURCES

### BOOKS

AULT, NORMAN. Seventeenth Century Lyrics from the Original Texts. London, 1928.

BARFIELD, OWEN. Poetic Diction. A Study in Meaning. London, 1928.

CARPENTER, FREDERIC IVES. Metaphor and Simile in the Minor Elizabethan Drama. Chicago, 1895.

CARPENTER, FREDERIC IVES. English Lyric Poetry 1500-1700. Selected with an Introduction. London, n.d.

CECCHI, EMILIO. Storia Della Letteratura Inglese Nel Secolo XIX, Milano, 1915.

CLARK, DONALD LEMAN. Rhetoric and Poetry in the Renaissance. New York, 1922.

COLLETT, HENRY. Little Gidding and its Founder. London, 1925.

COURTHOPE, WILLIAM J. A History of English Poetry, Volume III. London, 1903.

CROCE, BENEDETTO. Problemi di estetica e contributi alla storia dell' estetica italiana. Bari, 1910.

CROCE, BENEDETTO. Storia della età barocca in Italia. Bari, 1929.

EINSTEIN, LEWIS. The Italian Renaissance in England. New York, 1902.

ELIOT, T. S. For Lancelot Andrewes. London, 1928.

ELIOT, T. S. Homage to John Dryden. London, 1924.

ELIOT, T. S. The Sacred Wood. London, 1920.

EMPEROR, J. B. The Catullian influence in English lyric Poetry circa 1600-1650. Columbia (University of Missouri), 1928.

EVANS, JOAN. Pattern, a Study of Ornament in Western Europe from 1180 to 1900. Oxford, 1931.

FELLOWES, EDWARD H., CANNON. The English Madrigal Composers. Oxford, 1921.

FELLOWES, EDWARD H., CANNON and others. Edited, Tudor Church Music. London, 1922-29.

FRIEDERICH, WERNER P. Spiritualismus und Sensualismus in der Englischen Barocklyric. (Wiener Beiträge Zur Englischen Philologie, LVII Band.) Vienna, 1932.

GOSSE, EDMUND. Seventeenth Century Studies. London, 1883.

GOSSE, EDMUND. Shakespeare to Pope. London, 1885.

GREEN, HENRY. Andrea Alciati and his Books of Emblems. A Biographical and Bibliographical Study. London, 1872.

GRIERSON, H. J. C. Cross Currents in English Literature of the Seventeenth Century. London, 1929.

GRIERSON, H. J. C. The First Half of the Seventeenth Century. Edinburgh and London, 1906.

GRIERSON, H. J. C. Edited, Metaphysical Lyrics and Poems of the Seventeenth century. Oxford, 1921.

HAZLITT, WILLIAM. Lectures on the Age of Elizabeth. The Collected Works, Volume V. London, 1902-1904.

HOLMES, ELIZABETH. Aspects of Elizabethan Imagery. Oxford, 1929.

HODGSON, GERALDINE. English Mystics. London, 1922.

JULIAN, JOHN, D. D. A Dictionary of Hymnology. London, 1925.

KER, W. P. Form and Style in Poetry. London, 1928.

LATHROP, HENRY BURROWES. English Translations From the Classics. Madison, 1933.

MORTON, SISTER ROSE ANITA. An Appreciation of Robert Southwell. Philadelphia, 1929.

MULLINGER, J. B. Cambridge. Cambridge 1873, 1884.

MYERS, WELDON T. The Relation of Latin and English during the Age of Milton. [Dayton, Virginia] n.d.

NETHERCOT, ARTHUR H. Abraham Cowley, The Muses' Hannibal. London, 1931.

OSMOND, P. H. The Mystical Poets of the English Church. London, 1919.

PETRE, EDWARD Notices of the English Colleges and Convents Established on the Continent after the Dissolution of Religious Houses in England. Edited by The Reverend F. C. Husenbeth. Norwich, 1849.

PLEISTER, HANS. Die Worthaüfung im Barock. (Mnemosyne, Heft 7). Bonn, 1930.

PRAZ, MARIO. Secentismo e Marinismo in Inghilterra. John Donne-Richard Crashaw. Florence, 1925.

RALEIGH, SIR WALTER. Style (Second Edition). London, 1897.

READ, HERBERT. Phases of English Poetry. (Hogarth Lectures, 7). London, 1928.

SAINTSBURY, GEORGE. Edited, Minor Caroline Poets. Oxford, 1905, 1906, 1921.

SAINTSBURY, GEORGE. Edited, Seventeenth Century Lyrics. (Third Edition) London, 1900.

SCHELLING, FELIX E. Edited, A Book of 17th Century Lyrics. Boston, 1899.

SPINGARN, JOEL. A History of Literary Criticism in the Renaissance. New York, 1899.

SPURGEON, CAROLINE F. E. Mysticism in English Literature. Cambridge, 1913.

TAYLOR, RACHEL ANNAND. Aspects of the Italian Renaissance. London, 1923.

UNDERHILL, JOHN GARRETT. Spanish Literature in the England of the Tudors. New York, 1899.

WALKER, T A. Peterhouse. London, 1906.

WALKER, T. A. Admissions to Peterhouse. A Biographical Register. 1912.

WATSON, FOSTER. The English Grammar Schools to 1660. Cambridge, 1908.

WELLS, HENRY. Poetic Imagery. New York, 1924.

WHITE, HELEN C. English Devotional Literature (Prose) 1600-1640. Madison, 1931.

WILLIAMSON, GEORGE. The Donne Tradition: a Study in English Poetry from Donne to the Death of Cowley. Cambridge, 1930.

## ARTICLES

ALDEN, R. M. "The Lyrical Conceits of 'The Metaphysical Poets'." Studies in Philology, Volume 17 (1920), pp. 183-198.

BAROWAY, ISRAEL. "Spenser and the 'Song of Songs'." The Journal of English and Germanic Philology, Volume 33, (1934), pp. 23-45.

BEACHCROFT, T. O. "Crashaw and the Baroque Style." The Criterion, Volume 13 (1934), pp. 407-425.

BEACHCROFT, T. O. "Mysticism as Criticism." The Symposium, Volume 2 (1931).

BEACHCROFT, T. O. "Quarles and the Emblem Habit." The Dublin Review, Volume 188, pp. 80-96.

CHALMERS, LORD, MASTER OF PETERHOUSE. "Richard Crashaw, 'Poet and Saint'." In, In Memoriam A. W. Ward. Cambridge, 1924.

CONFREY, BURTON. "A Note on Richard Crashaw." Modern Language Notes, Volume 37 (1929), pp. 250-251.

FALLS, CYRIL. "The Divine Poet." The Nineteenth Century, Volume 93 (1923), pp. 225-233.

GREEN, HENRY. "On the Emblems of Geffrey Whitney of Nantwich of the Sixteenth Century." A paper read before the Architectural, Archeological and Historical Society of Chester. 1865.

HUTCHINSON, The REVEREND F. E. "The Sacred Poets." In The Cambridge History of English Literature, Volume VII, Chapter V. Cambridge, 1911.

KEMP, VIOLET. "Mystic Utterance in Certain English Poets." The Hibbert Journal, Volume 26 (1927-1928), pp. 474-483.

LEA, KATHLEEN M. "Conceits." The Modern Language Review, Volume 20 (1925), pp. 389-406.

MARTIN, L. C. "A Hitherto Unprinted Poem of Richard Crashaw." The London Mercury, Volume 8 (1923), pp. 159-166.

McBRYDE, JOHN McLAREN. "A Study of Cowley's Davideis." The Journal of Germanic Philology, Volume 2 (1899), pp. 434-527.

NETHERCOT, ARTHUR H. "The Reputation of Foreign versus Native 'Metaphysical' Poets in England." The Modern Language Review, Volume 25 (1930), pp. 152-164.

PRAZ, MARIO. "Robert Southwell's 'St. Peter's Complaint' and its Source." The Modern Language Review, Volume 19 (1924), pp. 273-290.

PRAZ, MARIO. "Stanley, Sherburne and Ayres as Translators and Imitators of Italian, Spanish, and French Poets." The Modern Language Review, Volume 20 (1925), pp. 280-294, 419-431.

READ, HERBERT. "The Nature of Metaphysical Poetry." The Criterion, Volume 1 (1923), pp. 246-266.

SCHIRMER, WALTER F. "Die geistesgeschichtichen Grundlagen der englischen Barockliteratur." Germanisch-Romanische Monatsschrift, Volume 19 (1931), pp. 273-284.

SHARLAND, E. CRUWYS. "Richard Crashaw and Mary Collett." The Church Quarterly Review, Volume 72 (1922).

THOMPSON, A. HAMILTON. "The Mystical Element in English Poetry.' In Essays and Studies of the English Association, Volume 8, 1922.

THOMAS, HENRY. "Three Translations of Gongora and other Spanish Poets during the Seventeenth Century." Revue Hispanique, Volume 48 (1920).

THURSTON THE REVEREND H., S. J. "Catholic Writers and Elizabethan Readers." Reprinted from The Month, December, 1894.

WALLERSTEIN, RUTH. "The Style of Drummond of Hawthornden in Its Relation to his Sources." Publications of the Modern Language Association of America, Volume 48 (1933), pp. 1090-1107.

WARREN, AUSTEN. "Crashaw and Peterhouse." The Times Literary Supplement, August 13, 1931, p. 621.

WARREN, AUSTEN. "Crashaw and Saint Teresa." The Times Literary Supplement, August 25, 1932, p. 593.

WARREN, AUSTEN. "Crashaw's Residence at Peterhouse." The Times Literary Supplement, November 3, 1932, p. 815.

WARREN, AUSTEN "Crashaw's *Epigrammata Sacra*." The Journal of English and Germanic Philology, Volume 33 (1934), pp. 233-239

WARREN, AUSTEN. "The Mysticism of Richard Crashaw." The Symposium, Volume 4 (1933), pp. 135-155.

WARREN, AUSTEN. "Crashaw's Paintings at Peterhouse." Modern Language Notes, Volume 48 (1933), pp. 365-366.

WILLIAMS, I. A. "Notes on Crashaw's 'Epitaph on a Husband and Wife'." The London Mercury, "Bibliographical Notes and News," Volume 7 (1923), pp. 411-412.

WILLIAMSON, GEORGE. "The Nature of the Donne Tradition." Studies in Philology, Volume 25 (1928), pp. 416-423.

# INDEX

# INDEX